THE
MYTH
OF
WU TAO-TZU

THE
MYTH
OF
WU TAO-TZU

SVEN LINDQVIST

Translated from the Swedish by Joan Tate

GRANTA

Granta Publications, 12 Addison Avenue, London W11 4QR

Originally published in Swedish as *Myten om Wu Tao-tzu*
by Albert Bonniers Förlag, 1967.
This translation first published in Great Britain
by Granta Books, 2012.

A CIP catalogue record for this book
is available from the British Library.

1 3 5 7 9 10 8 6 4 2

ISBN 978 1 84708 522 1

Typeset by M Rules
Printed and bound by CPI Group (UK) Ltd, Croydon, CR0 4YY

For Ci

But it is not altogether a matter of indifference that we do succeed, at any rate now and then, in spending our time in familiar intercourse with what we thought to be unattainable and longed to possess.

Marcel Proust, *Within a Budding Grove*

Preface

When I first heard the tale of Wu Tao-tzu as a child, entering a picture seemed a very natural thing to do. What else *could* you do?

Not to enter would have been to miss a golden opportunity. Pictures were few and far between in the 1930s, remember!

In Sweden there was in those days not a single television channel, no lush colour photographs in illustrated magazines, no coffee-table books full of eye-goodies and very few children's books.

So when I saw a picture that was more than a black smudge on the page, I jumped at it. Or rather, I jumped *into* it, as if it was a jungle to explore or a room to live in.

The pictures that most excited my fantasy were often those on tins. Tins of sardines, of meat or even of tropical fruit.

Opening the tin was opening the picture.

Smelling the contents brought me to the brink of the picture world.

Eating was entering.

*

As a schoolboy, a few years later, I had already lost this natural gift of entering into pictures. I now took what seemed to me a more realistic view of the matter. I prepared myself for a career as a practising magician.

An older friend, who was a professional and gave regular paid performances, showed me how some of his tricks were done. I used all my pocket money to buy a cloak, a wand and a top hat full of secret pockets.

Now when I heard the tale of Wu Tao-tzu my question was: *how did he do it?*

What was the secret behind the opening of the gates at the sound of clapping hands?

How did he manage the art of his own disappearance?

He seemed to have penetrated his painting and found an inner room, a liveable, habitable inner space, behind the surface of art. How was this illusion created?

Or was it, perhaps, not just an illusion? After all, the great German novelist Hermann Hesse spent his whole writing life trying to enact the myth of Wu Tao-tzu. Musil and Proust were not far behind.

The more I studied the myth of Wu Tao-tzu, the more I was fascinated by the possibilities it opened up.

Questions multiplied.

Why did he disappear?

What company did he leave behind?

Did he experience the culture of his day as desperate and meaningless?

Or was his vanishing an act of artistic self-confidence? An attempt to verify art in life?

Wu Tao-tzu had the courage for solitude. That is what is so tempting about his fate. He had the courage to disappear and continue alone, on the other side of the visible in art.

*

I have been on the look-out for Wu Tao-tzu all my life. I searched for him in China, in India, in Africa. On my last long journey I found his tracks in the deserts of central Australia.

Few deserts are so well taken care of as the Australian. Every stone, every bush, every waterhole has its specific owner and custodian, its sacred history and religious significance. Every holy place has its own holy picture.

The eternal truths of Aboriginal religion are expressed in the surrounding landscape.

The landscape is mapped in the holy picture.

Pictures and places have a peculiar personal intimacy.

You belong to them more than they belong to you.

It is your duty to travel to these places.

To care for them.

To paint the ground with the very pictures that map the ground.

You enter these pictures by painting your body with them.

You enter them by dancing them back into the ground.

You enter these pictures by dreaming them, by going to sleep in them, and sometimes even becoming pregnant by them.

You survive by keeping these pictures alive.

And by keeping them alive you do your bit to make the whole universe survive.

*

I write this from the roof of the Queen Elizabeth Hall, looking out over the City of London and what was once London's East End. I am sitting in 'A Room for London', shaped like the *Roi des Belges*, the ship Joseph Conrad captained on the Congo. It is a work of architectural art created by Fiona Banner and David Kohn, inspired by a work of literary art: *Heart of Darkness* by Joseph Conrad.

It is a room the Chinese painter Wu Tao-tzu could have entered after having clapped his hands.

It is a fully equipped bed and breakfast where he could have stayed the night.

It is even a room he could have lived in, if he had wanted to leave the world. Who would have come looking for him on top of the Queen Elizabeth Hall?

Down below is London, dark, glittering, full of mysteries.

I first got to know London through *Jack* London. It seemed utterly significant to me that the man who explored the abyss of London had the same name as the city whose misery he uncovered. That couldn't be just a coincidence, could it? I was only nine years old and anything was possible then.

Jack London's *The People of the Abyss* was one of the first 'real' books I read.

It was 'real' in the sense that it was not a fairy tale for children or an adventure story made up for boys. The Abyss really existed. Jack London had been there. He had resisted all the authorities who had said that it was impossible to go to the East End and still more impossible to stay there.

'To live there yourself,' his friends had said, disapprovingly. 'It can't be done, you know.'

Cook's travel agency would unhesitatingly and instantly have sent him to Darkest Africa or innermost Tibet, but to the East End of London, barely a stone's throw from Ludgate Circus, they knew not the way!

Finally, having burnt his boats behind him, he plunged alone into that human wilderness of which nobody seemed to know anything.

I came in secretly behind him.

*

'Nowhere in the streets of London may one escape the sight of abject poverty,' said Jack.

'It must not be forgotten that the summer of 1902 was considered "good times" in England. The starvation and lack of shelter I encountered constituted a chronic condition of misery which is never wiped out, even in the periods of greatest prosperity.'

'Following the summer of 1902 came a hard winter. Great numbers of the unemployed formed into processions, as many as a dozen at a time, and daily marched through the streets of London crying for bread.'

That I had never seen in Stockholm. I had never seen 'tottery old men and women searching in the garbage for rotten potatoes, beans, and vegetables.'

During the unemployment of the 1930s hungry men often came to our door asking for 'a boiled potato'. Always that same boiled potato. It was the proper, simple, humble thing to ask for. It was the proper, simple, humble thing to give. You could not refuse a hungry man his boiled potato. Poverty and unemployment had this utmost boundary: the right not to the rotten, but to the boiled potato.

As a child, I could always spot children from a poor family. For one thing, they wore a particular type of mittens that came in the church's Christmas charity parcel.

They also had a peculiar smell. Most Swedish working class families in those days lived in one-room apartments, with neither shower nor bathroom. So their children smelt of sweat and mould, of damp and dirt and overcrowding.

That was child poverty as I recognized it. But Jack London had seen 'little children clustered like flies around a festering mass of fruit, thrusting their arms to the shoulders into the liquid corruption, and drawing forth morsels but partially decayed, which they devoured on the spot.'

And their parents? What did their mothers say?

'The women from whose rotten loins they spring were everywhere', wrote Jack London. 'They whined insolently, and in maudlin tones begged me for pennies, and worse. They held carouse in every boozing ken, slatternly, unkempt, bleary-eyed, leering and gibbering, overspilling with foulness and corruption, and, gone in debauch, sprawling across benches and bars, unspeakably repulsive, fearful to look upon.'

'And I remember a lad of fourteen, and one of six or seven, white-faced and sickly, homeless, the pair of them, who sat upon the pavement with their backs against a railing and watched it all.'

And watched it all.

I couldn't help feeling that Jack London used the child's perspective to paint an unfair picture of these women, yes of all the people of the Abyss. Even so, Jack London's book made a great impression on me. When I visited England for the first time in 1948, what I wanted to see above all was the East End of London. I wanted to walk every street and enter every house mentioned in *The People of the Abyss*.

But they were all gone, bombed out. The abyss of war had obliterated the abyss of peace.

*

One of my early ambitions as a writer was to do a book about Wu Tao-tzu, using Jack London's method in *The People of the Abyss*.

His experiment had always fascinated me. It contained my

own story. But I wanted to repeat it in a different direction –
not descending into the abyss but ascending into art.

Where did Wu Tao-tzu go when the gates in the mural
opened? What did he do in there? What happened to him?

I can see it now. Literature has been really important to me
only as Utopia.

In my books, and not only there
but also in the hopes I have,
in my demands on life,
in the motives of my actions,
briefly – everywhere it may have practical consequences.

I discover the same presumption as in Hesse, in Musil,
in Proust.

As in the whole line of writers who have shaped me:
that art is not closed to man, that man can step into art.

The opposite of the East End is not the West End. But
where is it then?

I want to know how people are living there and what they
are living for. In short, I want to live there myself.

'Live there yourself?' said people with the most disapproving expressions. 'You can't, you know.'

It must be possible.

The prospect of a clearer and freer way of living has always
been held out to me in art and literature.

It must exist. Somewhere.

I've seen it in poems and pictures.

I've heard it in music.

There's a fearlessness there that makes my life foolish.

There are opportunities for happiness there,
that frighten me more than unhappiness.

There's an abyss in reverse and one falls upwards.

Why, then, do I live as I do?

Not even the professors at the university – scholarly men and women who without a moment's hesitation would have sent me to the darkest corners of the archives and the innermost petty details of the bibliographies – not even they could help me.

'Art as a way of living,' I tried to explain to them.

'Yes, of course! An excellent subject for a study of motifs.'

'But as a personal experiment?'

'What do you mean?'

'To examine the habitability of poetry. To live in a work of art.'

'Like you inhabit a house? You can't.'

'To test the ways of the spirit in practice.'

'That's – hmm – unprecedented. I don't think we can do anything for you.'

Clearly, I had to manage on my own.

Having burnt my boats I was now to enter a world about which no one seemed to know anything.

Like Jack London in the summer of 1902 in the city of the same name.

But in the opposite direction.

He stepped out of fiction, I wanted to enter.

He left his culture, I wanted to find the heart of mine.

I wanted to be present in the arts as they happen, an observer in disguise, an eyewitness of the spirit on the lookout for a better life than ours.

So I clapped my hands and started writing *The Myth of Wu Tao-tzu*. The first Swedish edition was published in 1967. It has never been out of print since then. The gates to the first English edition open here. If you ever dreamt of a bed and breakfast in art, here is your chance.

*

As I was celebrating my eightieth birthday in a ship on the roof of the Queen Elizabeth Hall, my old friend, the Chinese painter Wu Tao-tzu, came to see me.

He liked the strangely beautiful piece of habitable art where I was staying.

But the problem that was bothering him now was not how to enter art and live there.

It was the problem of feeding ten billion people.

It was the problem of fuelling five billion motor cars.

It was the problem of building two billion houses and apartments.

Our consumption of oil, paper, meat, etc. cannot be multiplied by the population of the world.

Natural resources would come to an end in a few decades, in some cases months.

The effects on the global climate would be disastrous.

We have created a lifestyle that makes injustice permanent and inescapable.

We have created a world where robots produce robots. Where capital breeds capital with very little need for the Eastenders of the world.

Tell me what will happen when the majority of mankind has become technologically superfluous.

At the same time rebellious with hunger and economically unimportant.

What will then stop a final solution of the world problem?

In *The People of the Abyss* the Eastenders already saw it coming.

They are, Jack London wrote, 'encumbrances', of no use to anyone, not even to themselves. 'They clutter the earth with their presence and are better out of the way'.

The poor themselves felt there to be 'a wise mercy' in 'sending them over the divide'. In 1902, they already had a language for it. A dose of 'black jack' or 'white potion' would 'polish them off', they said. All agreed that the poor person who gave too much trouble would be quietly killed.

Jack London's East End is 'the world as I found it' in the first 'real' book of my young life.

At the heart of the world's darkness there was this quiet, peaceful genocide, accepted and agreed to even by those who were the next to be killed.

Sven Lindqvist
London
March 2012

Originally commissioned by Artangel and recorded as 'A London Address' in the *Roi des Belges* on the roof of the Queen Elizabeth Hall, 29 March 2012. www.aroomforlondon.co.uk

1

The Tang Dynasty painter Wu Tao-tzu one day stood looking at a mural he had just completed. Suddenly, he clapped his hands and the temple gates in the picture opened. He went into his work, the gates closed behind him and he was never seen again.

There is often talk of empathy in art, 'living' in it, the power of projecting oneself into it, but rarely in any practical sense. Usually only small children understand what that is all about. I think you haven't 'made your way' into a work of art until you have been guilty of the banal mistake of confusing fiction with reality. Again and again, I have made that mistake myself, particularly when it comes to *The Glass Bead Game*.

In the Western Mountains outside Peking there is a cave containing a gilded sculpture of Buddha. Its expressive face is said to be that of a real man coated with a thin layer of gold. Anyone listening can hear his heart beating.

That legend expresses the same dream – of being inside what can really be regarded only from without. The art is nothing but gold dust brushed over reality to fix it. Below the surface is a living human being, enclosed and preserved by the golden film.

It was my own heart beating in his body. So I often found it difficult to leave the place.

For a long time that immobile hovering bird of his face.

For a long time that golden peace, enclosing him as if behind the eyelids of a sleeping man.

*

Curriculum vitae.

I was born at the end of the New Age, just before the Dark Ages began to return.

I had a wife and children, house and garden. I wrote my books, was considered an amiable writer and lived at peace with the world. I travelled in Europe and India. Everything seemed to be in order.

Then the summer of 1914 came.

My education began. The so-called 'great times' had broken out.

My friends are perhaps right when they say that ever since then my writing has lost its beauty and harmony. What are beauty and harmony when you are running for dear life between crumbling walls? I am beginning to believe that all my artistic endeavours have been a mistake.

But that is unimportant. My mission, what I once called my mission, no longer exists. I see my task, or rather my way to salvation, not in poetry or philosophy, nor in any speciality. But only in this – to allow the crumb of life and strength still left in me to live its own life.

That is where I am today. But the past often fills me more than the present, nor can I clearly separate what is to come from what has already been. I live very much in the future. So I need not end my autobiography here, but will calmly continue.

I occupied myself largely with painting and Chinese witchcraft, but then turned increasingly to music. I was gradually approaching that period in life when there is no point in developing or modulating an already more than sufficiently expanded personality. Then you are faced with the opposite task: to allow your valued self to go under in the world.

So I put my work aside and turned entirely to practical magic. Even if my artist's dream had been in vain, I was a born magician. I had already travelled far enough along the paths of Lao Tse and I Ching to be able to know that reality is incidental and transformable.

At seventy years of age and with honorary doctorates from two universities, I was finally arrested for seducing a young girl by witchcraft. In prison, I asked permission to be allowed to paint.

This was granted.

I painted a little landscape on my cell wall.

The landscape contained almost everything I have taken delight in during my life. Mountains and rivers. Seas and clouds. Widespread forests. A small train was in the middle of the picture, hauled by a steam engine. It was approaching a high mountain and the engine had already begun to enter the tunnel.

But the prison guards would not leave me in peace.

Finally, I thought the time had come to put an end to these torments. If I was not to be allowed to go on with my innocent artistic games, I would have to make use of the serious arts to which I had devoted so many years of my life.

For a moment I stood there, holding my breath.

Then I politely asked my guards to wait while I boarded the little train in the picture to look for something.

They laughed and allowed me to do so.

So I made myself low and stepped into my picture, boarding the little carriage and going with the train into the tunnel. The steam from the engine poured like a cloud out of the tunnel opening and hid the picture. When the smoke had dispersed, the picture had gone.

The prison guards remained there in great confusion.

*

On the train.

Gently swaying, softly thumping like a steamer. Signalling like a great ship in fog. The snow envelops the endless plain in a white night.

The general is reading. The widow has painted herself and is standing in the corridor. We are still carrying our own time with us like snails, but day and night have merged into each other. I don't know when to become sleepy, or when I shall be hungry. In the middle of the day, darkness falls in the white night. In the middle of the night, the sun rises, pale and unborn, enveloped in the foetal membranes of the snow-smoke.

I have feared this cold. The air would fasten to my skin like cold iron against the tongue. My nails would blacken, my eyes water and be sealed by ice. But the cold is not festering, nor strangling – it is laughing. Every join in the blue rail sings out like a steel pick in frozen ground. Sun above high, wood-white snow-gates. Haymaking winter with verdant loads. I would be able to confide in this cold, sleep through an ice age and wake in order to wash my flushed face in snow.

The sun rises, white as the yolk of an egg in winter. Treeless plain, treeless mountains. Schoolchildren on their way across endless fields of snow.

*

When the general had finished his book, he stayed sitting for a long time in dreamy silence, turning the pages, perhaps seeking an explanation for some mystery. A long time has already passed since he left the train.

Out on the plain, a lone man with a yoke is carrying two pails of ice-cold water through this desert of snow.

The sun. Day after day or night after night, this white eye stares at me.

Falling over treeless plain, treeless mountains. Schoolchildren on their way home across endless stubble fields. A shimmer of gold in the air. Sunset in Siberia. Nothing overdone, just a single bright red colour in the black and white.

The Chinese comrades are playing chess by the light of a naked bulb. I rest my eyes. The general was after all from my world, from my day, the kind of person I understood. But in these stern faces I find nothing personal, nothing acquired. Although outwardly open, their eyes remain inwardly closed and inaccessible.

They are playing. The board has bulged and the squares look like uneven stones. White knight below black castle. Darkness has fallen.

*

Dawn.

Golden glow in the darkness. The horizon sharpening. Snowy ground growing lighter.

Upwards in continuous bends as if we were circling round the same empty, light-filled bowl. Upwards! Emerging light from below on the landscape gives a unique feeling of height. Far down below us lies the mist in the valleys: ground clouds.

The sun comes out. Grazing horses raise their heads. Ice glints at the bottom of the bowls. Further and further around us. Stronger and stronger feeling of being lifted.

Here people are dressed in full-length costumes, scarlet and saffron yellow. The houses appear to be designed by eighteenth-century futuristic architects: past and future are stones in the same arch. Sun-grass as newly fallen manna over the ground.

During the night we pass the last border. Ravines of rain-water. A loose, near-landsliding mountain landscape. Mountains in transit, on their way downwards like water. Future plains, today disguised as mountains.

And the people: eroded like their land, like their mountains. Nose almost rained away. Eyes silted together. Their movements ground down as if by water, their language with no inflected forms, only a few sounds: worn down, low.

Gravestones in groups on the plain, like chimneys in a ruined town. Milestones measuring the desert of time.

Slowly, slowly, as if driving a flock of sheep ahead of us in the dusk. Hither and thither in the darkness as when you spin round in blind man's buff. What will happen now? Where will we come to? Pointless questions, hypotheses with no basis. Too tired, far too tired. Time destroys all wounds. A peasant in spirit is worth ten in the forest. There – the flames of a steelworks in the darkness! Slowly, slowly, like a hovering bird with one wing in the past, the other in the future, and the present like the thumping heart in my own body, endlessly slow the train passes through the suburbs of Peking.

*

Hermann Hesse writes in *Curriculum vitae* (*Kurzgefasster Lebenslauf*) that he painted a small landscape on his cell wall and disappeared into it. Stepping into art – that is a theme throughout his work. Nearly all his heroes vanish like Wu Tao-tzu.

For Steppenwolf, it is music which opens a door to 'the heart of the world' and the cool, light, hard smiling wisdom of the immortals. With the aid of wine, drugs and 'magical theatre' he is occasionally able to go through that door. The novel ends with him disappearing completely into these spheres. 'Mozart was waiting for me' are the last words in the papers he left behind.

This penetration into art is particularly clearly described in *Journey to the East* (*Die Morgenlandfahrt*). The central character of the story is Leo, servant of travellers to the East, representative of the spiritual upper world which the narrator, H.H., seeks in vain to enter. On the last page of the book, H.H. finds a little sculpture, a strange double figure combining Leo and himself, back to back:

> Inside the figures I saw something moving slowly, extremely slowly, in the same way that a snake which has fallen asleep moves. Something was taking place there, something like a very slow, smooth but continuous flowing or melting; indeed, something melted or poured across from my image to that of Leo's. I perceived that my image was in the process of adding to and flowing into Leo's, nourishing and strengthening it. It seemed that, in time, all the substance from one image would flow into the other and only one would remain: Leo.

In all these cases, the step into art is surrounded by powerful elements of mystification. One does not flee out of a secure prison on a painted train. Anyone who takes drugs in order to live in the way Mozart played is closer to the mental hospital than to the sphere of the immortals. Hesse is offering symbolic descriptions of an inner event, while at the same time suggesting, with all the arts at his disposal, that they can be put to practical use.

This suggestion is strongest when the theme appears for the first time, in his unfinished novel *House of Dreams* (*Haus der Träume*). This is about an old man. He is standing by the rose bushes. It is time to tie them up.

He is standing in his garden, where no gaze from outside can penetrate. In it, everything is the fruit of his own dreams and cares, based on what he has taken over, filled with growth and future, but impossible to complete.

The world has contracted, he thinks with the trace of a smile.

Since he left his employment, he has spent all his days in his garden. There he prefers to be alone with his thoughts, increasingly taciturn, increasingly sunk in the greenery he is creating and tending. Even to those closest to him, he has become closed and inaccessible. After his evening meal, he disappears into his Chinese room. Sometimes he sits all evening quite silently in the darkness out in the greenhouse.

Have you never read the Chinese stories? he asks. In them it is often the case that, after an active and useful life, one night a man just leaves his house and fields, his wife and his servants, his work and his books, and disappears. His time has come.

A disappearance of that kind is already slowly on its way for the old man. His stillness will soon become complete silence. He has begun to go up into the 'life of things'. He tends his flowers, but not in order to show them to anyone. He thinks his thoughts, but not in order to relay them. His life is contracting, condensing and merging into his garden.

'What do you think is most important?'

'Simplicity.'

He is an artist about to disappear into his work. So he becomes more and more indifferent to his art. He simply reads the Chinese classics and Goethe's late prose.

'A thousand compositions and paintings I previously could not imagine living without I am now quite indifferent to. One single book, one single piece of music would be enough.'

'Which piece?'

'Bach's *Actus Tragicus*. Or *Ave Verum Corpus* by Mozart.'

'You could just as well name twenty other pieces of the same rank.'

'Admittedly. That was sentimental of me. Naturally it would do just as well without Bach and Mozart. Without art of any kind. Art is a thin and sensitive skin between us and the heart of the world. To reach the heart, you must also finally penetrate that reach skin.'

His far-seeing eyes laughed . . .

*

That is where the manuscript ends. This was in August 1914, and the war took Hesse by surprise in the middle of his far-seeing smile. He broke off from his work and wrote an article on the task of intellectuals in war.

I would be the last to deny affinity with my native country, he wrote. I have no desire to prevent soldiers from doing their duty. But my duty is another.

The first casualty of war is the truth. Does a Japanese drama become worse because the Japanese fleet has shelled Tsingtao? Has a bad German book become superior to an English book because those countries are at war? Does the outbreak of war make French culture worthless?

That is what they want us to think. We must refuse to participate in this deceit.

It is understandable that politicians and soldiers are blinded by hatred of the enemy. But when intellectuals are also seized by warmongering and write battle poems, boycott 'enemy' art and defame whole peoples – who will then defend the truth?

Goethe did not write war poems in 1813. He retained his own inner freedom and followed his intellectual conscience. Anyone who has once believed in the idea of humanity, in the universality of science, in art with no national boundaries, must not betray his conviction now that it is being put to the test. If intellectuals betray spiritual values, war will destroy the foundations of Europe. Someone must uphold peace even if the whole world is at war. Someone must attempt to preserve as much peace as possible – that is the task the future poses today.

That is what Hesse wrote. This article became the decisive demarcation line in his life. It condemned him to exile and made him a great writer.

It is almost moving to see how unsuspectingly he steps straight out into the abyss. The article is polemical but at the same time trusting. It appeals to a solid bourgeois fellowship of values. It breathes a strange assurance, which shows that Hesse has not understood the forces he is challenging. He expects to be heard and respected. Only a month previously, any such declaration of neutrality of the spirit would have seemed obvious, even idyllically pointless. But German nationalism now fell upon him like a wild beast.

All he was trying to do was to apply the old gardener's way of life to an actual political situation. One single step outside the garden – and his spiritual super-world burst like a bubble.

*

The dream of stepping into art is still there. But what had been a means of attaining becomes a means of escaping. The old man's smiling road to fulfilment becomes a desperate last way out of the prison of reality, away from the razor of the suicidal. The garden motif shrinks into an azalea on the stairs up to Steppenwolf's rented room – it no longer represents a possible way of life. The disappearance is no longer the crown of an active life in bourgeois solidarity. Steppenwolf has seen through it. Behind its beauty and harmony, he sees anti-Semitism, anti-communism, jingoism – seeds of a new and much more terrible disaster.

When that disaster became reality in the 1930s, Hesse reacted in fundamentally the same way as he had in 1914. He wrote *The Glass Bead Game* (*Das Glasperlenspiel*). The introduction, describing how intellectuals unite and create their own world beyond bloodstained history, was published in 1934, shortly after Hitler took power. In it, Hesse presents in fictional form the same exhortation he had addressed to the intellectuals of Germany at the outbreak of the First World War. Hold out! Your resistance groups are small, isolated, impotent – I know that. But you must not give up! You are the ones to preserve for the future a sense of truth and conscience.

And when even this appeal turned out to be naive, in about 1938 he began writing the central part of the novel. The biography of Joseph Knecht, one of the clearest and strongest fictional dreams of wish-fulfilment ever written, was created during Europe's darkest years. It consummates the theme interrupted by the First World War and gives final shape to Hesse's vision of man's ability to step into art.

*

The connection between *House of Dreams* and *The Glass Bead Game* is clearest in one of the novel's minor characters.

I am thinking of the peculiar episode of 'The Elder Brother'. He is one of the learned and original loners usually to be found in Chinese institutions at European universities. He once studied at St Urban's and there outdid the best teachers of calligraphy and interpretation of the ancient texts. He drew attention for his keenness to appear Chinese, even outwardly. He insisted, among other things, on addressing all his superiors as 'My Elder Brother', an expression that stuck to him as a nickname.

He devoted himself most of all to the oracle game of I

Ching, which he carried out in a masterly way with the traditional yarrow sticks. Twenty-five years ago, he went south and planted a bamboo grove which protects a carefully tended Chinese garden from the north wind. There he has created a strictly ancient Chinese idyll and lives at peace with himself and the world, occupied with meditation and the copying of ancient scrolls.

So that is where Joseph Knecht goes. He arrives at the Bamboo Grove late one afternoon and steps into a rare garden, with water running in wooden pipes from the well to a stone-walled pool, where a couple of goldfish are swimming in the clear, still water. A thin bespectacled man in a greyish-yellow linen suit is squatting by a flower bed. He gets up and slowly approaches, not in an unfriendly fashion, but with the awkward shyness of a recluse. He looks at Knecht, waiting for him to say something. Not without embarrassment, Knecht speaks the Chinese words of greeting he has prepared: 'The young disciple takes the liberty of paying his respects to Elder Brother.'

Knecht is permitted to stay at the Bamboo Grove. He helps to collect firewood and tend the garden, he learns to rinse brushes and grind Indian ink, to keep an eye on the weather and handle the Chinese calendar. Most of all, he studies I Ching and learns the oracle game with yarrow sticks. But whenever he tries to bring other matters into the conversation, he meets with only deaf ears and some Chinese proverb: 'Dense clouds, no rain'.

*

This was the bamboo grove I wished to visit. Chinese was studied in Stockholm as a dead language. It was stepping into a world of ancient words of wisdom on rice paper. They laughed at me and left me to it. I took the train and got off in

Peking, prepared to swim like a goldfish in the world of paintings and proverbs that I loved.

On the very first Sunday I was already at the palace museum.

There was a flower there from Ming. Pale, light, fragile – but hovering.

And the pictures of bamboo, where the passing instant enters infinity – a stylized pattern re-emerging again and again with the freshly experienced vividness of the moment.

But most of all the pictures from the Sung period. Those landscapes vanishing into a silken dusk, almost absorbed into the fabric, sunk into their own background, as light as if painted with mist. I remember a few peacefully grazing horses, individual and yet together, calm creatures in gentle movement. You see only one of them from the front, his head raised. His mane and tail are white. They are white in an intense, watchful way. He has heard something, far away, he is listening – and what he is listening to becomes a sound that suddenly penetrates the whole picture.

When we came out of the gates, the cry had ceased. The shafts pointed upwards, empty, the reins thrown down on the road, mare and foal in the ditch, between them membranes and blood. The foal was still trembling, white vapour enveloping them in the clear cold January day.

*

With fifty sticks, roughly the contents of an ordinary matchbox, the following experiment can be made.

One stick is put aside. The others are divided at random into two bundles. From the right-hand bundle, a stick is taken and clamped between the little finger and the third finger of the right hand.

Then take the left-hand bundle in the left hand, while with

the right hand pick the sticks four at a time until four or fewer remain. These are put between the middle finger and forefinger of the left hand.

The right-hand bundle is counted in the same way and the remainder put between the middle finger and forefinger of the left hand.

Then there are either nine or five sticks altogether in the left hand. These are put aside and the same procedure is carried out with the remainder.

This time there are either eight or four. The combined number of three calculations decides the first of the six lines of a hexagram, which after eighteen calculations can be looked up in the *I Ching*.

This is the stick oracle which the Elder Brother lays in front of Joseph Knecht in the Bamboo Grove. The result of the calculation becomes a hexagram called *meng* and the judgement is as follows:

Youthful folly wins success.
I do not seek the young fool.
The young fool seeks me.
At the first oracle I provide enlightenment.
If he asks again there is trouble.
If he makes trouble I provide no enlightenment.
Perseverance furthers.

Knecht has gone to the Bamboo Grove to study the *I Ching*. The name means 'The Book of Changes'. In its present state, it is an immensely complicated collection of texts on various levels. But at its core are sixty-four hexagrams, each one of which represents an abstract concept. The concepts are arranged in a meaningful way, 'not without a certain inner consistency and artistic force', to quote Joseph Needham's understatement in *Science and Civilization in China*. The principle of the dialectical movement, intensification through transition between opposites, is a feature throughout – just as in *The Glass Bead Game*. The sequence of concepts is intensified in a spiral towards 'truth' and 'fulfilment', but ends, like the novel, in 'chaos, possibility of perfection'.

The glass bead game arose from a game with multicoloured beads on children's abacuses. Even the *I Ching* had a modest origin. In the days of Confucius, it seems to have been a kind of peasant almanac, a collection of popular folk wisdom that came to merge with one of the many books of fortune-telling of the day, and was expanded into a comprehensive method of predicting the future. But with the interpretations and commentaries over the centuries, the prophecy element has been pushed further and further into the background and the material has been given poetic form and ethical content.

Most of all, the *I Ching* became a repository for Chinese scientific finds. Needham relates this to the bureaucratic Chinese social order (which also prevails in *The Glass Bead Game*) and calls it an 'administrative' approach to nature. Just as a certain type of task is to be referred to a certain official, so the Chinese scientists referred their discoveries to one of the hexagrams in the *I Ching*.

This method of organizing knowledge did not lead to a technical conquest of reality, as our research into natural laws did. But the *I Ching*'s view of the world is superior as an artistic fabric of relations between minute events in everyday life, distant astronomical and physical facts and high ethical principles.

On one important point, the *I Ching* has influenced Western thinking. Leibnitz, one of the glass bead game's predecessors, got to know about the book through Jesuit missionaries. It inspired his invention of binary arithmetic, and perhaps also his theory of the predetermined harmony of the world.

Modern research into the *I Ching* as meta-science has as yet scarcely begun. But it is certain that the book offered a system of symbols which came to include all Chinese knowledge of nature and an important part of their proverbs and poetry. It constitutes an attempt to refer all spiritual activity to a few intercorrelated fundamental concepts. It is a glass bead game.

Which can be played with the contents of an ordinary matchbox. The matchstick calculations are not only a harmless fool's stereotypes. They are a meditative technique to bring to mind and incorporate a whole view of the world. What separates the oracle book from our fortune-telling is its artistic form and intellectual superstructure. What separates it from our poetry and knowledge is that it is intimately connected with a plan of spiritual exercises. In this combination of poetry and practice lies its unique value as a symbol in *The Glass Bead Game*.

*

I Ching commentaries in Peking central library.

On the way home. A flock of birds rises from the roof of the palace. The surface of the water in the moat is touched with cold and becomes ice, disappearing into the mist far away in the south. Light sky, dark earth. All round me, crowds of workers cycle past – the street slopes, the hubs humming as they freewheel.

This is what surrounds the *I Ching*. Humming hubs and flocks of thousands of birds rising and heading north. The library catalogues and rows of scholars below dim lamps. I exchange a word with a mechanic. He leaves me immediately.

Although we are going the same way, he is now walking over there on the other side of the street.

Cold. Brisk walk. The pale blue trolleybuses, fully laden and almost motionless, pass the stillness of the moat. The pedestrians preserve their breath behind face masks. Darkness falls swiftly and the mass of birds vanishes northwards across the white sky.

*

A drop of water falls into the hollow of the ink-stone. The ink-cake looks like a domino. I move the ink-cake clockwise against the stone with swift, smooth, circular movements and catch the scent of pine. Once the ink is thick enough, I dip the wolf-hair brush into it and write.

Write with a too flowing brush – the paper absorbs the ink immediately and a blurred uneasy line arises. With too slack a brush, the line bellies. With too weak a brush, the lines become crabbed or ragged. With uneven pressure, the characters acquire 'grandmother's feet'.

My teacher – in the early 1960s, during the great crisis, you could find a teacher of calligraphy by reading the notices on the Peking telegraph poles – so, my teacher writes before me. The simple parts of the character: the dot, the horizontal line, the left swing, the perpendicular line, the vertical hook, the right swing and right hook. He writes the character for 'eternity' and a few more basic characters.

His movements are calm, disciplined, free.

Each stroke is irretrievable. Alteration is a mortal sin and a child can spot it. So in calligraphy it is often a matter of waiting, but never hesitating.

I rush on – fumbling for the swiftness and sure touch that seem so temptingly close. Laboriously and clumsily, I struggle over the paper, fall down, thud, blot. Years of work lie ahead of me. I want to be bold, individual, myself. But here, I realize at once, there is no possibility of any self not based on complete control of the basic stroke.

Calligraphy is not an art for the rebel. It is based on disciplined spontaneity, inconceivable without rules and doctrine. The doctrine is the sum of tradition: a way of performing. Mastery consists of achieving freedom in relation to tradition. And freedom consists of a kind of assimilation of the rules agreed on, so that no decision from above is necessary. Judgement can be left to the hand.

The fact that the actual tool makes such demands must have influenced the writers. No intentions force the soft brush. All effort works against its aim. To be unerring in the handling of a tool of this kind requires practice which schools the whole person.

It is said that at seventy years of age Confucius was able to follow his heart's desire without relinquishing what was right. Not exactly a piece of information I set much value on. He probably had little desire left to relinquish. But it must be understood that Confucius also wrote characters. In the end, he was able to practise the entire exhilarating freedom which tradition offers the master. As he moved the brush, he could follow every caprice without the line ever becoming coarse. Nor did it become vague.

Our script has no such opportunities. (Have our lives?) Perhaps that is why we have had to create so much literature, and a literature in which the paradoxical pride in every work is to be unlike all others. I think that for long periods the Chinese chose calligraphy before poetry because it gave them greater enjoyment to make use of a poem rather than to write a new one. On any material, it was possible for calligraphy to provide a creative experience.

Our lettering lacks utopian range. But wherever you may fall over, there is also a potential balance. Chinese script spans the entire register, its wealth of forms allowing for sensitivity, strength and that combination of both which is called maturity.

Will any of the lifestyles of our day provide space for such maturity?

*

The question can be settled only by practice. The Chinese know by tradition how this is done. Everyone cannot be allowed to do it in his own way. If the order of strokes is not right and the movement of the brush not correct, the character will never be good. One fault in the basic line is enough to thwart the entire result. There is no way out of a faulty starting point.

The brush has to be held perpendicularly. The teacher must not have forbearance – that would be criminal. The pupil will thank him for his strictness when method has become second nature but will never forgive a tolerance that allowed his individual deviation to pass. For precisely that deviation will in future lie like a stone in his wing, making perfection impossible.

To be allowed to make mistakes is not freedom. Only perfection provides freedom.

The teacher's upright brush dances over an old page of the *People's Daily*.

('So a newspaper can be used in two ways?'

'Yes. One can write characters on it. And one can give it to the waste-paper collection.')

Unhesitatingly, knowing without choosing, in secure, impersonal and yet utterly revealing movements. No one else could have written it. His handwriting is his own just as his face is. He can disguise it but not change it. His handwriting is the accumulated result in which years of practice, events and thoughts have been immeasurably recorded.

Call it compliant firmness. Call it rhythmic force. The brush moves. It apparently always starts in the wrong direction but bends nimbly and takes the ink on in the direction of the stroke. These are still only the first exercises, those which have to be repeated every day. They still have little to do with the organization of the characters, nothing yet said about the degree of blackness, about the unity, the rapid simplifications and unexpected connections between strokes. This is just the obvious foundation with neither too much nor too little. But that is also the crown of the art.

You cannot even write badly without knowing what comes first.

But this is also the very last thing you learn to perfect.

For perfection does not consist of a few drills and additions. Like in the baroque lute music, everything amounts to the right touch, and progress consists of an increasingly profound understanding of the significance of that touch. It is usually called the alpha and omega of an art: a spiral-shaped movement in which again and again you have to return to the starting point, but then on another level, and it is the transformation of this starting point which makes perfection.

This demands total concentration, which has to be quite without tension. (Why does one spot a learner driver before one even sees the L-plate?) Will-less, without tensing a single muscle, you concentrate all your attention on this basic point and then deliver everything over to your hand.

You no longer support the arrow once it has left the bow, runs an old saying.

So write nothing on the first day. Just look at the character and let it sink into your consciousness. Don't write on the next day either. Just wait and let your desire work until the knowledge has penetrated throughout your entire body.

Wait until your hand knows it.

And nothing else.

Wait until your hand is empty and everything else has fallen out of it.

But when your entire consciousness embraces the character and nothing else – then grind the ink, pick up the brush and give your hand the freedom of your heart. And with one strong blow, as if from the tail of a fish, your 'self' has vanished.

It is in your hand that everything has to be. At every moment, it chooses between a thousand possibilities. It is too late to issue orders. It is not the time to explain. Whatever does not exist stored as experience in your hand is useless. What at that moment does not go up into the movement is irrelevant. Your will can only block. It is useless to draw in air and pump yourself up. It can happen only by itself. We want to draw inside what is beyond our control and thus force it. But what is best will never allow itself to be forced. That can be achieved only in the way the calligrapher achieves it.

*

From Lung Ting, we could see in the distance through the sand-fog one of those high camel-like bridges for which the Chinese are rightly famous.

In the construction of a bridge of that kind, two potential disasters must be taken into consideration. The mass of stones in the bridge tautens like a bow. It can happen that the ends of the bow slide outwards so that the bridge collapses. The Chinese insure against this with strong vertical abutments.

The second potential disaster particular to these bridges is that all the tensions in the bridge are transmitted to its weakest place – the crown of the span. It has to resist enormous pressure from below – as much as the entire accumulated pressure of the forces lifting the span. So the danger is that the weight of the stones presses the highest point upwards and the bow snaps.

Only the Chinese have created a bridge that risks collapsing upwards.

2

Later on, Joseph Knecht described the months he spent in the Bamboo Grove as a happy time; yes, as 'his first awakening'.

He continued his Chinese studies and was particularly keen to expose himself to ancient Chinese music – the classics praise music as the primeval source of all order and beauty. He had already got to know their wide moral concept of music through his old Music Master, who might actually be said to embody it.

Since leaving his post, the old Music Master has been living a life of retreat in his garden pavilion at Monteport, becoming more and more silent and taciturn. Those around him at first think it is his hearing that has deteriorated, but it turns out that he can hear just as well as before. They also think that perhaps he has become distracted in his old age and can no longer focus his attention. But others say that he has somehow already departed and is living increasingly in a world of his own.

Since this absence began, his voice has grown softer and his handshake feebler. All his last strength has been gathered into his gaze, which is more inward-looking, more secretive and insistent than ever. His silence is the radiant end-station of a life that has been free of coercion but full of devoted work, and full of music.

In his youth, he chose music as one of the paths to the highest aims of man, to inner freedom and fulfilment. Since then, he has done nothing but allow himself to be permeated by music, letting himself be transformed by it, right from his humble clever pianist's hands and his enormous musical memory to every part of his body and soul, to his pulse and breath, sleep and dreams. He has become a form of manifestation, a personification of music. So his death is becoming a process through which the dust disperses, the bodily functions disappear and life increasingly accumulates in his gaze.

When death finally comes, Knecht finds the old man lying on his bed, his little face shrunken 'to a rune and arabesque, a magical figure no longer, but nonetheless testimony to complete happiness'.

*

It's the truth – I was not afraid. And yet I felt ill at ease, as two incompatible demands were being made of me which seemed to be splitting me in two. I was being put on exhibition while the whole situation demanded solitude. One part of me wanted me to amuse the spectators and another was ordering me not to bother about them.

The silence meant that something special was expected of me. The pause put me under an obligation.

Although my arms, legs, head and body still obeyed me, at the same time they added something extra, something quite unnecessary. I wanted to place my hands and feet naturally, but they made certain flourishes of their own, and that resulted in a pose – like at a photographer's.

Strange! Although I am an ordinary, natural person, I simply couldn't sit still, and behaved like a bad actor. Theatrical falseness was closer to me than genuine naturalness. They said afterwards that my expression turned stupid and I looked guilty.

'Let's go on now,' said Tortsov, after I had been tormented

enough. 'But we'll eventually come back to these exercises and learn to sit still.'

'Teach us to sit?' the pupils said in wonder. 'Wasn't that what we were doing?'

'No,' replied Tortsov firmly. 'You weren't content just to sit still.'

'What should we have done, then?'

Instead of answering, Tortsov quickly got up and walked in a businesslike manner over to the chair, then sank into it as if he were back at home.

He neither did nor tried to do anything, but nonetheless he drew our attention to himself. We followed him with interest, wanting to know what was going on inside him. He smiled; so did we. He turned thoughtful and we really wanted to know what he was thinking about. His eyes fastened on something and we felt we must see what had attracted his attention.

Tortsov interested us although he ignored us completely. Where did the secret lie?

He replied, 'Let's repeat the experiment. Maria, come over here!'

Maria was placed on the chair and nervously started moving. Tortsov stood beside her, looking with concentration for a note in his notebook. Gradually, Maria calmed down and finally sat quite still, looking with attention up at Tortsov. She was afraid of disturbing him and was waiting patiently for the instructions to come. Her posture became natural.

A moment went by. Then the curtain fell.

'How did you feel?' said Tortsov.

'Me?' she said, not understanding. 'Were we acting?'

'Of course.'

'But I thought I was just sitting waiting until you had found in your notebook what we were to do.'

'That's just what was good. You weren't acting. You really were waiting for something, and then it became art. Activity, motion, action – that's art.'

'But excuse me,' said Maria, 'I was only sitting still.'

'Immobility is not the same as passiveness,' Tortsov explained. 'Physical immobility can be the result of a powerful inner action. The value of art is determined by its spiritual content. So I'll change my wording a little and say this: In art, action is necessary – internal or external action.'

*

Among the thousand Buddhas, I saw many with insolent, lecherous mouths. Fat, debauched faces, slack smiles, swollen heads, knobbly brows. Sullen, pouting mouths, contemptuously jovial with screwed-up noses. The V-shape in particular made them look malicious, and in some the eyes and eyebrows continued slanting wedge-shaped upwards and outwards over the tops of their heads. On others the gold leaf had flaked off and the worm-eaten contents looked out as if from a helmet of holiness.

Some have creases in their faces like duelling scars, and small frizzy beards. Sometimes the face is only a village at the foot of the huge mountain of the brow. On the obese ones, the faces well out, the mouths a shaft in the flesh. On the ascetics, on the other hand, the cheeks hang slackly, their bony hands thrusting the world away as if playing an invisible piano, their chins curving like a wood shaving in the fire.

One of the holy men slits open his face. Out of his external face, he takes an inner one, folding it to one side like a cloak. Beside him Bacchus swings his goblet. His beard is heavy and as rounded as a bunch of grapes. Those sunk in golden sleep sit surrounded by the emperors of holiness. The peaceful ones are those embedded. Number seventy-eight is playing the flute. Another leans forward as if to gaze intently at something inside him.

But most of those I saw were nothing but lively urchins, smiling behind the golden draperies at the corners of their mouths, scratching the little gold pearl of their Adam's apples.

Not until Lung Men, outside Lo Yang, did I find anything of what I wanted to see.

In Lung Men, there are thousands of caves cut out of the mountainside, some as big as town halls, others just small crypts or niches. And caves are carved into the sides of the caves, resembling boxes in a vast theatre, the sculptures an audience sunk in holiness.

Buddha everywhere. He sits surrounded by thousands of images like a king with his stamp collection. He is as small as a pinhead. He is immense and has square toes at which a man can sit at table. The variety of format makes a powerful impression – the small are nothing but a map over what is larger than they are.

On a plateau, three gigantic Buddha figures are at different stages of composition. You can see the first rough carving with its series of parallel blows. Then detailed carving in which the inner form begins to appear beneath the rough granite-like surface. The central figure is complete, the skin of its face sandpapered, dune-soft right into the sharp fold of skin in the incision of the eye and the huge bow of the eye socket.

The third time in Lung Men. The cave of the great Buddha. The swallows, those light and wind-swift birds of the moment, swarming round that smiling face gazing out over the still, mud-sluggish river.

Below it a bridge being built.

Everything led to the expressionless calm of his face. The grotesquely muscular watchmen standing furthest out, the Hercules motif of Buddhist art. On each side of Buddha, admirers crowd in magnificent diadems and massive hanging earrings, bejewelled necklaces and heavy pendants fastened across breasts with a buckle. Jewellery. Magnificence. But all this is only to lead us on.

Behind Buddha the mountain is in flames. The halo has four courts, the outermost blooming, the innermost radiating. The simple folds of his garment spread out like circles in the water. They are all but forecourts to his face. The closer, the more bare is the stone. The silence of the face is the end-station: inner freedom and perfection.

I had tried to approach the Music Master with Stanislavski's methods. I had analysed Hesse's technique as he builds up his character. Was that just a series of literary tricks? Or could it teach me something about what was possible to experience of his state? I had followed that smile via Siddhartha back to the Buddhist legends. And here I was.

On the way home: a worker's hands. Tool hands, hardened and as if freed from his body. Especially the nails – thick and flat, gleaming at the end of his fingers like slices of jade.

*

Skilled high jumpers know how to let the centre of gravity of their body pass *under* the bar, while joint by joint their body passes *over* it.

This method is used in many literary works so effectively that even in the most brilliant achievements the centre of gravity scarcely moves vertically.

General Kiggell, Chief of Staff of the British Army during the First World War, was the first of the staff to dare go out into the battle zones to see for himself the reality in which his orders were carried out.

He burst into tears.

I have a feeling that many writers would do the same if they had the courage to approach the reality in which their words are enacted.

Has Hesse been there?

Certain connections are absolutely clear. In *The Glass Bead Game*, the character of the Music Master strongly resembles the old man in *House of Dreams*. The garden theme and the 'Chinese room', beloved by this old man, reappear in *The Glass Bead Game* in the form of the Bamboo Grove frequented by the loner.

The old man in the *House of Dreams* fragment from 1914 reads only two things. Whatever in him inclines towards Goethe's late prose becomes the Music Master. What inclines towards the Chinese classics becomes the Elder Brother.

But Hesse himself? Can he do what Tortsov does in *An Actor Prepares* – come forward and show how it's done?

Hesse is found in his autobiographical poem *Hours in the Garden* (*Stunden im Garten*), published in 1936. *House of Dreams* was published privately that same year. And Hesse was in the middle of working on *The Glass Bead Game*.

Hours in the Garden forms the mediating link between the two works, the most important resting place on the motif's long journey between first draft and final version.

And there we also meet Herman Hesse, a bespectacled man in a yellowish-grey linen suit and a straw hat, friendly but shy, hunched over the flowers in his garden in Montagnola.

*

Towards seven o'clock every morning
I leave my study and step

Out on the bright terrace.
Here my tools lie ready and waiting.

(*Morgens so gegen die sieben/ verlass ich die Stube und trete/ Erst auf die lichte Terrasse./ Hier liegt und wartet mein Werkzeug.*)

His tools: a mattock and a basket for weeds. Between wood and steel, he has slipped in a piece of shoe leather, following the advice of a wise old Tessinian. The mattock ought to be kept damp so that the handle doesn't loosen – it is always needed.

With basket and mattock in hand, he sets out on his morning walk – towards the sun ('*der Sonne entgegen*'). Climbing roses and granite, grass and weeds in profusion. Greeting the flowers by name. A stranger was also there, a huge cactus by the steps, as tall as a ten-year-old. During the previous winter, the snow had snapped its fleshy branches.

With his hat pressed down over his forehead, he walks round the stone steps of his garden, entranced. For a moment his eye is still tempted by the distance-blue mountains. In the morning they have a remote faintness, then they become more massive during the day, drawing closer and expanding in the brilliance radiated by warmth.

But then again he turns his eye to the ground, where the soil is to be weeded and the stepped paths kept in order.

This is on the terrace by the stable, indeed not a stable, but called so all the same. Here, my friend, buried in the greenery, you do not rule over proud vistas. You have gone.

By the stable wall is the old compost heap from the year before last – dark, porous earth, a treasure ('*dunkle, lockere Erde, ein Schatz*') – decorated with sunflowers nourishing themselves on the rich earth, to give back in the autumn what they have taken.

The life cycle of plants is swift in its slowness. In spring regarded as touching and amusing children. Then suddenly one late summer's day mysteriously different, weighed down by secrets, ancient and tired, and yet superior in their smiling maturity.

The well. The vegetable garden. And the tomatoes on the south wall. I can reveal a secret. Damp, loose peat moss and a touch of artificial fertilizer. Try it! It pays off.

Stakes of chestnut from woods nearby, but some plants have soon grown beyond them. For as among people, there are some which shoot to the skies more greedily and ruthlessly, sometimes admired for their size and strength, sometimes laughed at for their strange unquenchable aspirations.

Are those stakes steady and straight? Take the string out of my pocket and gently tie the tops to the stake. Always a pocket full of string. Others use raffia. That looks better.

But I never lack string; I save it from the parcels
Of books publishers send to my house every day.

(*Mir aber war an Schnur niemals Mangel, die Bücherverleger/ Senden mir täglich Pakete ins Haus, deren Schnüre ich sammle.*)

The shadows have gone, the weeds in the basket wilted. The sun blazes. Seek shade in the grass by the hedge along the road. Peasant women in heavy shoes. Their laughter and laments. This green hiding place, this friendly refuge. Often when I am driven from my work by despair, defeat, letters from someone full of hate and by my own inability to live. But received here and made happy.

Many dreams and thoughts.

The happiness of losing yourself.

But received here lost and made happy in dream-thought.

But received here in dream-thought lost and made happy.

A place for living between idleness and industry, for playful action without labour. Making a fire and burning dead weeds. This inclination towards fire. A boyish desire? Or a kind of sacrifice? Every habit, virtue or vice, is rooted in the primeval. And this? A chemo-symbolic cult which means reunification of manifold to unity. Branches and grass to ash. Helping the dead to be sooner at home ('*Helfe dem Toten rascher entwerden*'). And I myself return, meditating, the same way from manifold to unity. Like the alchemist over his fire, seeking to refine the metal, going through the same transformation inside him, until after days and weeks of practice his mind, like the metal in the crucible, had been freed of the poison and was gleaming.

Oh yes, my good friends, you laugh. Patience. So, matches and a little paper. In the autumn, a flaring open fire, but now in the warmth a covered, quietly glowing pile. This is my simple faith – through fire, the soil can be renewed and made fertile. Have that from Stifter, where the gardeners 'burn' various kinds of soil. So mix the waste with earth in the pile and find dark and light, red and grey ashes – the fruits of many charred hours, contempt for time and inward-looking forgetfulness.

Forgetfulness of duty.

But the passion to improve others and educate the world must also be mastered. Our life is so constituted that the desire of noble spirits to make history, as all other urges, ends in blood and violence.

Wisdom?

Alchemy and games. The good nature to oppose the course of the world, even in times of threat and need, that peace of soul the old praised and strove for:

let us do good
without a thought of changing the world;
even so it will pay.

(*und tun wir das Gute/ Ohne an Änderung der Welt gleich zu denken;/ auch so wird sich's lohnen.*)

The silence of the heat through small sounds. Kneeling and filling the riddle with ash and earth. And falling below the riddle in an even rhythm, filled with music from the memory, though as yet with no name, but suddenly: Mozart, a quartet with an oboe. And out of the music rises the playful thought called the glass bead game:

> In times of joy
> it is play and happiness,
> in times of need and confusion
> it is my guide and comfort.

The little hill is growing, the sifted soil running out through the riddle. Serve the reeking pile and again fill the riddle. Flowering suns below the stable wall. Hearing music, seeing people past and future, wise men, poets, scholars, artists building a cathedral of the spirit – to describe some day later, the day not yet come, or never ...

Someone is calling from the house: my wife, who has returned from town, goods and chat. Next time you must come with me to the barber. You mustn't let your hair grow all down your neck.

In the end, one is human.

*

Children.

The sun rises over the Shantung peninsula, though that is not what you should look at. At sunrise, you should look west and see the colours of the ground in the low light. The shadows are long at sunrise, but so is the light – softest and warmest nearest to the ground. Plains and hills unite in the same even swell.

Dark peasants. White fields. A lone stone gateway to something long since vanished. A gateway through which flow only fields.

The peasants work with mattock and spade, sod by sod of the poor stone-burdened soil of the Shantung peninsula. Always manually. I never see them ploughing with anything but children.

There may be as many as ten children. So a man harnesses ten children to the plough and starts ploughing.

Endless, infertile, winter-hard dry soil. A father is to plough and harnesses his children to the plough. I don't really know how anything of that kind can be said in order to give it its full significance. I don't know what happens in China. But I know that on this beautiful February day a Chinese father had nothing else but children to harness to his plough.

The train rushes on. Mountains of light, dazzling fields.

*

Giving yourself over to a small world. Going into it. Creating a reality into which to disappear. Letting the hedges be the picture frame. Stopping there.

Your gaze leaves the distance-blue mountains and returns to the ground, to what you are doing, to where everything is familiar and many times repeated. The perspective of eternity is the life cycle, biological and spiritual – antiquity of the future. Earth, sky, sun, shade, water, vegetation – eternal things. A world that desires nothing but itself. Might then possibly be the string from the publisher's parcels of books. Or a haircut at the barber's. For in the end, one is human.

These humorous admissions simply stress the sufficiency of the garden. Idyll is the art of fulfilment. It is sufficient.

His tools lie there waiting. The mattock with its piece of

leather. 'The mattock ought to be kept damp so that the handle doesn't loosen – it is always needed.' The poem has a know-all didacticism which is partly feigned, partly real. The idyll traditionally needs the wealth of detail, sun-drenched expert knowledge. Hence these Hesiodian growing secrets. But Hesse does not seriously try to teach me how to grow tomatoes. He just happens to have tomatoes handy and makes them the excuse, not to mention other much-loved excuses, to teach me something else.

Idyll is the art of happiness. But the image of happiness cannot be skimmed off the objects reflecting it. So happiness has to be made concrete with this exhaustive simplicity. Here it is totally embedded in the slow, unhurried presentation of the facts. The spiritual content of the poem is rooted in its practical advice and hints. It is the recipe as an art form. And the sense of tangibility is transmitted from the feigned didacticism to the real.

What Hesse describes is a series of metaphorical actions. He is tending both a garden and a universe. He sits by his pile like an alchemist at his crucible, like the glass bead player at his characters, and burns the manifold of weeds into the unity of ash.

The weeds of life to the ash of art.

Living weeds to dead ash.

Dead weeds to fertile ash.

All the possibilities of the game are there in his work by the fire. His work is a metaphor, but one that can be accomplished. An art that has become an action.

That is the core of the poem, its real message. I have tried the method myself and know that it is practicable.

*

In 1951 I wrote *Journey at Home*, attempting to carry out *Hours in the Garden* in a Third World setting.

My starting point was the impossibility of changing the corrupt society attacked in my book *Advertising is Lethal*. The alienation in such a society. The necessity of a simpler way of living.

Water.

Food.

Gardening.

Etc.

Metaphorical action as a solution to the problem of alienation.

Metaphorical action as a solution to the problem of inactivity of art.

Seeking out your social situation in its concrete form and working on it – the only way to make your conscience effective.

Seeking out artistic problems in feasible actions – the only way to make what is spiritual practical.

A synthesis of Mrs Cliff and Father Rodion – the social and the meditative forms of activity.

One single experience described does not allow itself to be assimilated into the game: the visit to Agios Isidoros. But I didn't understand that until in China – well, not really until on my way home from India in the summer of 1963.

*

Idyll, Schiller says in his famous essay on naive and sentimental poetry, is the ideal of beauty applied to real life.

Idyll describes a free unity between inclination and duty, characterized by an utter lack of conflict, both within the individual and within society. The contradiction between ideal and reality which provides material for satire and elegy (as poetic forms and ways of life) has vanished here. Calm is the predominant mood of this form of literary genre – not the calm of inertia but the calm of perfection, a calm which reflects not emptiness but fulfilment.

Though just as all resistance ceases, it becomes incomparably more difficult than the two other genres to produce *movement*, without which artistic effect is inconceivable. Idyll has to be the satisfaction of the soul – without, however, the cessation of striving. Solving this problem is the task of a theory of the idyll, according to Schiller.

In *The Glass Bead Game*, the actual game is the highest expression of a union of stillness and movement.

The game is portrayed as perfected, as the culmination of a great cultural tradition, a conclusive codification of it. Just as the Chinese calligrapher does not devote himself to inventing new characters, the Castalians do not try to create new cultural values. They use those which already exist. In the game the players continue bringing these values to life and thus keep them in movement, alive.

We seek movement by expanding, they by using.

There is a definitive limit to the quantity of cultural material a person can avail himself of in an active functional manner. The personal discipline of the players and the construction of the game mean that this saturation point for a Castalian is immensely high. And what else is needed? Which movement in which direction would be preferable to complete freedom of movement within the existing human tradition?

It is sufficient.

But where does the human being go? The problem of movement in the idyll entails a paradox that can be formulated in this way. Meaningful movement means that one is on the way somewhere. The idyll, as Schiller defines it, intends to describe a state of fulfilment. Where should a person in that state go?

Why should a state of that kind need to be changed? It is perfect. But in that, it is also emptied into a still life. And if it is difficult to describe perfection as standing still, then it must be even more difficult to live it. A state with no meaningful movement becomes a kind of death. That cannot be regarded as perfect. So the concept itself appears to contain a contradiction, and that is what Schiller calls the idyll's problem of movement.

In *House of Dreams*, Hesse tries to solve the problem by introducing movement on the periphery. The son comes home. The mother is worried. The brother is wrestling with problems. His wife is in despair. These conflicts take the narrative onwards while the stillness of the old man deepens in the centre.

In *The Glass Bead Game*, Hesse goes in the opposite direction and makes the periphery stand still. Joseph Knecht passes through the Bamboo Grove, passes through the garden of the Music Master. He himself does not stop. He lives in a static society, but he himself is constantly changing. He penetrates further and further into Castalian secrets. He rises higher and higher within the hierarchy. The problem of movement is solved through a cross between Utopia and a 'Bildungsroman'.

Or rather – the problem has only been postponed.

For what happens when Knecht has reached the top of the hierarchy, when as a man he is equally finished as the culture he is playing with? Is the only thing left for him to follow the masters and let himself sink down into that great stillness?

Steppenwolf does end with Harry Haller stepping into the life sphere of great art. But Knecht is already there. *Journey to the East* does end with H.H. becoming Leo. But Knecht himself is Leo, the servant – where is he to go?

He leaves art and goes out into the world.

*

THE MYTH OF WU TAO-TZU

I can't point to any specific event.

It could have been during an evening in Tokyo in the summer of 1961. I was on my summer holidays from Peking University and was just about to go back to China when Mr Mumson turned up.

A sympathetic American of my own age, his jacket hanging from his forefinger, though his name seemed odd. He wondered whether I would contribute something towards increasing understanding between the USA and China.

We happened to bump into each other at the temple market. He was catching goldfish with a small sugar net that dissolved in the water. A common market amusement in Japan. You can have as many fish as you can catch before the net dissolves.

All understanding, said Mr Mumson, has to rest on knowledge.

A stream of images ran through my head. I could think of a great many things America would need to know to achieve greater understanding of China.

Could I, for instance, Mumson asked me, remember whether the Peking–Shanghai railway was electrified all the way?

Were there any Chinese naval units assembled anywhere near Shanghai? Had I ever seen or heard mention of transports of unusually large, oblong containers?

Oh, so you haven't.

He did not want to talk money.

That was a dreary subject. But naturally my expenses would be paid.

And his government realized I would be running a certain risk. Even if only an insignificant one. So a regular monthly salary might be considered.

For really valuable information, there would then be unlimited possibilities of paying according to merit.

I needn't worry. No secret radio transmitters. No invisible ink. Only to spend a week together. Why not in Switzerland? Over pleasant conversations.

I gratefully declined.

Only a 'suggestion', said Mumson politely. He pronounced the title of my first book in broken Swedish.

A cultivated person. And thorough.

They had read my books, he said. They believed I was really on their side. Perhaps more than I knew myself. I would soon be thirty. The time had come to go out into the world and take a stand. He spoke particularly about intellectual freedom. I ought to think the matter over.

In that way Mr Mumson, point by point, made me think it over – just where would I really side with the USA? It was a useful exercise, and disheartening. Why hadn't I done it before? Why had I simply brushed aside the Chinese statements as meaningless propaganda? What kind of intellectual glass bowl was it that kept me imprisoned like a goldfish?

It became an uneasy night. In the morning, Mumson phoned to ask me if I had changed my mind. I had not.

*

Or perhaps the experience of the masses, the almost constant feeling for three years of the pressure of the masses. Clearest in Shanghai, as it's a European city. You wake in the morning and think Stockholm has been invaded by 10 million Chinese. It was Chinese New Year and everyone was out on the streets, imprisoned by each other – for several hours we were jammed into the crowd, helplessly made to follow with the stream as inch by inch it was pressed on between the walls of the houses. That was the first time. Like being in a hydraulic press. There is a distance round the concept of the individual. Our culture arose in small Greek city-states, among loners in Iceland, in a still sparsely populated European archipelago. There is a *noli-me-tangere* in the European sense of self that the world has no room for. No one can refuse to accept another's body against his. 'COMRADES! WALK CAREFULLY! COMRADES! MIND THE CHILDREN! COMRADES!' The loudspeakers kept hammering continuously against our eardrums. It was anachronistic to try to live a personal life in our day. When Edgar Snow interviewed Chinese communists in the 1930s, he found they lacked biography. They could not remember their private lives. They had perhaps not experienced anything else but collective events. I remembered that frightening me – but how long is one really to go on celebrating one's birthday? Why have I always thought that what happens to me is somehow more significant than what happens to other people? 'COMRADES! DON'T PUSH! COMRADES! WALK CAREFULLY! COMRADES!' With mechanical regularity the monotonous, impersonal, utterly expressionless voice hammered its message of care into the crowd, which with infinite slowness was pressed on between the walls. It took a couple of hours. It took a couple hours to press out of me the feeling of being something special, a different person, with a destiny of my own.

Afterwards, back in the hotel room, naturally it returned, but not in the same way as before. Never really quite the same.

*

Or perhaps when at last I managed to get into the philosophical poison cabinet of the university library.

The catalogue listed an excellent collection of modern Western philosophy, but no one appeared to have read the books. I tried to borrow some, but they were kept at the institution. And there the caretaker would not let me in.

In the end I went back with the professor of the subject. There was a great palaver by the front door, but he was, after all, the professor.

Then we walked along the ground-floor corridor and went into a kind of office. Some blue-clad men, far too rough to be librarians, were sitting there, drinking tea. Something evasive had already come into the professor's explanations and I think he was regretting his promise.

At the door of the reading room once again identification was demanded. Inside, the walls were filled with Marxist-Leninist philosophy in Chinese and Russian. Some students were reading magazines. In one corner was a barred booth, a kind of cage, and in the door sat a girl taking cuttings out of the *People's Daily*.

She let us in. And there they were – Moore, Russell, Carnap, Wittgenstein – the lot.

I had not thought about how dangerous these books are. In a society with thought-control, they are quite literally lethal.

How many times had I, with their help, not put my finger on that point where the Chinese may not think their thoughts to an end but are derailed because dogma and reality come into conflict? And that not only in obvious crackpots but also in very sensible people. There is a trip-point they can't get past.

When they kept bringing up the history of imperialism and the misery of the masses, I tried to get them to ask more precise questions. I steered the conversation away from the state of the world to propositions such as 'The existence of poisonous weeds is an objective reality' or 'The policy of the Party is correct.' What really was a poisonous weed in literature?

'A book which harms the work of building socialism.'

'Who decides it's harmful?'

'The people.'

'How do you know what the people think?'

'The Party knows.'

'And if you analyse in the same way the sentence "The Party's policy is correct"?'

What would he reply? It was pleasing to carry on reasoning of that kind. The awareness of intellectually controlling the situation gave me a sense of security and a clear conscience.

'Under what circumstances would you admit that the Party's policy is not correct?'

'That's inconceivable.'

'So the sentence is a tautology?'

'No ...'

'Then you must be able to say under what circumstances it would be wrong. When would the Party's policy be wrong?'

'If it deviated from Marxism-Leninism and the thoughts of Mao.'

'Who decides if it deviates?'

'The people.'

'And the Party knows what the people think and so the Party itself decides that it's correct, is that right?'

The trip-point.

But where was that point in myself? Where do I start denying obvious facts? At what point do I refuse to draw the conclusion of what we all know?

I suddenly thought that they were only apparent victories I had won in these debates. It was too easy. My thinking was constructed in order to find these weak spots, but what was it made to conceal?

As I stood there leafing through those familiar books with the professor uneasily stumping back and forth, I thought that I somehow recognized this room. You could by all means be allowed in, but you simply didn't go there. What do we lock up to escape realizing what we already know?

I already knew. It is the history of imperialism. It is the misery of the masses. It is the state of the world.

*

Joseph Knecht finally dives into the clear mountain waters. I bathed in Hai Dian.

A bath in the Hai Dian bathhouse costs a few pence. In winter, I went there to get the floor-cold out of my body, in summer to get rid of the mask of salt that had settled on my face.

When you open the door, you see the back of a large mirror – the old wall against evil spirits still there in the semblance of another function. There is also a common comb.

The great hall is crowded with cupboards and benches. The men lie resting, covered with bath towels, or sit talking, many of them with a long brass pipe in their mouth. We all drink boiled water. My bedmate is a young cadre in uniform. As we undress, we chat about feet. He has trouble with his, the skin won't stay put and is peeling off right up his shins. Then we go into the washroom.

There you can borrow a large cake of green soap and wash yourself under the shower. There is a pissoir in the corner and a kind of slippery bench smelling of soap which is used as a washboard when you scrub yourself.

The pool, the common bathtub, is divided into rectangular compartments as large as family beds. At first you sit on the edge with your feet in the water, dip your flannel in and let the water run over your body. The water is the same for us all, public and opaque. But it is only tepid in the outer beds, hot in the inner. You slowly make your way inwards. There you sink down to your neck and soak yourselves like packed plants in a forcing bed.

Afterwards you wrap yourself in a bath towel and go out into the hall, where it is wonderfully cool and fresh. A serving comrade brings hot facecloths. Snores and a quiet murmuring are heard all round. You lean back and enjoy the weight of your own body. Red banners with slogans are stuck on even the skylight.

It is all pleasantly sybaritic in a simple and wholesome way. But this isn't just enjoyment. The world comes very close to you in that Hai Dian bathhouse. Water carries feeling better than air. What you feel comes closer than what you see. All these bodies, scarred by war and pox, worn out by hard work, thin from lack of nourishment, with grotesque varicose veins, blackened legs and skin diseases – they are all alive and feel as my body does. When the same water encloses us, it is easier to realize this.

Lying beside me was a worker with the blood running down his legs in the huge bumps of his veins, his swollen genitals floating by his knees like a vast reddish-black aubergine. Then an old man without the strength to open the door. That skeleton came slowly crawling over the edge and sank into the water. Thin, fragile arms. Skin hanging loose over his back, beneath it the sinews like a system of strings in some toy invented by children. At every movement this tangle of threads would tense and lift skin from bone. His rump was a small brown wrinkled patch hanging where his legs were inserted into his body.

I have seen similar things on photographs of the starving in the world. But then we weren't lying in the same water.

'LONG LIVE GREAT UNITY BETWEEN THE PEOPLES OF THE WORLD' says the banner on the skylight. Inside my young, Swedish, newly bathed body, as it enjoys its own weight, I can still feel the weight of an old Chinese worker's body.

3

The distinguished of Calcutta still live in Alipore. An eternal Sunday peace lies over the large white villas in their great gardens. And like a lock on the entrance to this part of the city is the Alipore Court, in which today a gang of murderers is being tried.

The forty-nine murderers sit behind bars as if in a cage at the zoo. But the courtroom is so crowded, they could reach out their hands and strangle every one of us from behind. They are all dressed in long white shirts as if for baptism. They understand nothing of the procedure, which is being carried out in English. But now and again one of them is brought forward, his hands clasped, to answer questions in his own language. An official interprets for me in a whisper.

'Did you shout, "Kill that man"?'

'No. I'm innocent.'

'Did you throw yourself over the wall into the factory area to start fighting?'

'No.'

'Did you swing an iron bar around?'

'No.'

'What have you to say?'

'Nothing. Yes, I was standing in the queue in the coolie-line. Then they came rushing up and attacked us.'

'Who?'

'The factory manager and his hired men. They shouted, "Now we'll kill all those union people." They hit me on the head. I woke up in hospital.'

The clerk gets up and frees his hands from prayer. Puts his fingerprint on a document. Sinks down again behind his barrier of tattered yellowing papers.

Dry coughs. Rustling paper. The whirr of the ceiling fans. Voices grinding on in a language incomprehensible to them, determining their fate. To no one has it occurred that the murderers need an interpreter.

Their vacant looks wander through the open doors of the court. The factory manager's black car is parked outside, the driver asleep in it. In the middle of the yard in a small pool of blood lies a dead dog.

One after the other, the men are called out.

'Is it true you attacked the new workers brought in during the strike?'

'No. I was just about to eat. I was standing cleaning myself outside the coolie-line. I saw a whole lot of people rushing at me, throwing stones. The factory manager had a gun in his hand. He pointed at me and cried, "There he is!" I woke up in hospital.'

The factory manager is sitting beside the prosecutor, a large middle-aged man with forceful features below his curly hair. Behind him are his workers in the cage, so close they could stick their hands out and strangle him. The row of gentle, dreamy faces, murderers' faces with vacant frightened eyes. Men of an alien class are deciding about them in a foreign language. They understand nothing but the names. When a name whistles through the air, an eye gleams. But no one knows whether his name means hope or despair.

*

On the third day of the trial, counsel for the defence rises.

'I REPRESENT,' he shouts in quite a different tone of voice

from that used before. The courtroom falls completely silent as the sharp voice cuts through the air. Everyone sees his accusing forefinger, trembling with suppressed indignation, directed first at the prosecuting counsel, then at the factory manager. He is acting for the men in the cage. They don't understand what he is saying. But he uses his voice and his gestures so that they understand that someone is forcefully pleading for them.

'I REPRESENT,' he shouts, 'forty-nine unfortunate men who have fallen in the battle between rich and poor.

'They had requested better pay and the factory management crushed them. In this court, the company has been given the honour of appearing as witnesses for the prosecution. But it is the representatives of the company who should be behind bars. Today, in this court, counsel for the prosecution does not represent society. He is representing a company.

'My learned friend, counsel for the prosecution, has been very thorough over how many witnesses identified every single one of the accused. But with not one word has he explained that all these witnesses are employees of the company.

'Only sixty to a hundred workers took part in the disturbance, we are told. But where were the others? Did they see nothing? Did they hear nothing? Did they have their hands over their eyes ...?'

The judge: 'They were wise men. They kept out of the way ...'

'Yes, wise indeed. Wise enough also to keep away from the courtroom. They didn't want to lose their jobs by testifying against the company. And where are the strike-breakers? Who were they? Where have they got to? Seventeen injured were taken to hospital, where their names were taken down. But none of the new men was among them. So not one of them was injured? Why has not one of them testified here? And why are there no outside witnesses? Your worship, with respect, I beg to submit that if anyone merely stumbles in the street, hundreds of people gather round ...'

The judge: 'All you need do is to stop and stare up in the air ...'

'Precisely! And where are all these people in this case? Why has not one testified?

'We have heard trained, drilled witnesses. I deeply regret my learned friend's attitude. He is trying to act compassionate and wishes to free certain men on the grounds of insufficient evidence. But this whole testifying farce we have heard here simply demonstrates one thing: it has been the wish of the company that certain people should be picked out.

'My learned friend has had the good grace to ask why the workers have not sued the company, if it was true that they were attacked and maltreated. I shall answer him. Immediately after the event, these men were taken away by the police. Most of them have been in prison for months. All have become unemployed. None has any money. How could they take the company to court?'

The judge: 'But perhaps the union ...?'

'The union, your worship, was precisely these men and they were accused of murder, as the police have taken the side of the company. The police should have arrested the real criminals instead. The police should have at least commenced an immediate investigation and taken statements from those present at the time. The police ought to have collected and bagged the weapons said to have been found there. The weapons counsel for the prosecution is now producing – what do they prove? They could be any old bits of iron. All of the prosecution's material evidence proves one thing only – that the police are working as tools of the company.'

After a glance at the clock, the judge interjects: 'Perhaps we could continue tomorrow ...'

'I request that tomorrow I may claim yet one further hour of the court's time. I need no more. In a case in which all the witnesses are company employees, in which the police have lost the sketches of where the bodies were, in which the company is allowed to draw up a false plan over the factory area to support the prosecution's testimony and the prosecution nonetheless cannot make up its mind whether the crime was committed inside or outside the walls – in a case such as this, I do not think I need claim an excess of the court's time to arouse doubts about my learned friend's case.'

The judge: 'Court dismissed.'

The men in the cage are taken away.

Are they innocent? The question appears to be totally irrelevant. I have seen the factories and the workers' living quarters. Of course wild-cat strikes do occur at places of this kind. Of course trouble arises when strike-breakers are to take the sleeping places of the dismissed men in the coolie-line. Of course the police have to take the side of the company. All that is inevitable. Everyone knows why it's inevitable. It's a quite different matter the court has had to try today – the least interesting in this context.

The drama is over. It was about forty-nine men who didn't understand what was being said. The actors were three lawyers in black gowns keeping a piece of Europe hovering between them for a few hours. Now the curtain has gone down and they are standing around laughing in a small group by the court doorway. The voice of the counsel for the defence has returned to normal. The driver has woken up. Everyone gets into the factory manager's black car, which is skilfully steered round the dead dog and disappears into Alipore.

For the distinguished of Calcutta still live in Alipore. An eternal Sunday peace lies over the large white villas. This morning I happened to sneeze by the open window and the gate-boy flung his hand to his eyes in salute. Wandering musicians make their monkeys dance to rapid drumbeats. Servants clad in white walk their masters' pet dogs. The established order rests secure beneath the giant pillar-like palm trees, which appear to bear up an unaltered and unalterable class system.

*

'Why did you lose the election?'

'My opponent made great promises.'

'What did he promise?'

'Tax relief for the landowners.'

'Can he actually do anything?'

'Nothing.'

'What's the most difficult problem in the constituency?'

'Not enough land.'

'Have the land reforms been carried out?'

'No. It's shameful to have to admit it. We wanted to proceed cautiously and not offend anyone.'

'What are you doing to get your voters back?'

'We have three hundred members out in the district explaining to the voters that they were wrong.'

'Is it the few influential people or the voting masses who decide the election result here?'

'The few take advantage of the poverty and dependency of the many.'

'Bribe them, you mean?'

'Direct bribery does occur. But what is more important is that the voters are politically ignorant. And that's because far too few, only about 1 per cent of the population, took part in the struggle for independence.'

He had been in prison for ten years under the British. It had made him into an ascetically well-controlled and self-righteous man. Not voting for him is to have been 'wrong', a moral failing.

What is the difference between a thief and a politician? The Indians reply that the thief steals first and goes to prison afterwards. It is the other way round with the politician.

He was a merchant. But his competitors did not like him exploiting his political influence in business. Now he devotes all his time to politics, is totally identified with the Congress Party, enveloped in the aura of the great leaders. Gandhi, Nehru and Tagore gaze down at us from gigantic photographs in his spartan study.

We talk for an hour. He replies directly but often impatiently to questions. He does not allow himself to be provoked by silence. A man who knows all the tricks, even those of honesty, and does not hesitate to use them.

It occurs to me that truth and falsehood are to him like two sides of a knife, so close. What is important is the edge – power.

*

His successful opponent, Dr Sinah, non-party, lives in a white villa on the other side of the road.

At eight in the morning he is sitting in his tropical rose garden, the gate open and a stream of people coming in and out. Dr Sinah is having his breakfast and receiving clients. Rubber stamp and ink pad, fountain pen and prescription pad lie on the little table. He prescribes medicine for one, a recommendation for another.

'What do the people demand of you as a member of parliament?'

'That I should be accessible. No guard on the gate, as you see. As I am a doctor, people have a reason for coming to see me, and I know everyone. Otherwise I wouldn't have won the election. Most of those who come have individual requests that have nothing to do with politics.'

'What can you do for them?'

'Recommendations. Children to schools, adults to work. Not that it's much use. I mostly settle disputes in the villages. The political struggle in the villages has very little to do with programmes and principles. It's based on old squabbles between different village factions. One party promises to take on the problems of one side and so local squabbles are elevated to political problems. Democracy has come too soon to India. That's my private opinion. In twenty years' time, perhaps ... But some progress has been made. Previously, a candidate could guarantee a majority by convincing one or two powerful men in a village. Now an election campaign has to go into rather more depth.'

'What did your campaign cost?'

'Eight thousand rupees. Posters, pamphlets, transport to the polling stations and tea for voters who had long journeys.'

'In what way is your political programme different from that of the Congress Party?'

'It isn't. I told you, this isn't a matter of programmes. Theirs is good, but they have no intention of carrying it out. Corruption flourishes openly and goes unpunished. The rich circumvent the laws. "This man is one of mine. Make an exception for him." Not a square foot of land has been distributed to the landless.'

'But things are improving?'

'In a way. The sick are not so sick as they were fifteen years ago. The rich have become much richer. I myself am a good example of that! All development plans favour the rich. They pay for more and more elaborate theatre performances. The surplus from the land does not go back into the land but is wasted. Those who work the land don't own it. That's got to be stopped, otherwise production will never increase.'

'All big landowners must be against you for those views?'

'No, on the contrary. Most of the landowners voted for me.'

'What? Do landowners vote for those who want to take their land away from them?'

'Oh well,' he said. 'They know I'm not the one who decides.'

He might just as well have said they know I am not really serious. They know my views are only well-meaning but at heart irresponsible eloquence. They support me, despite my radical ideas, in order to put pressure on the Congress Party – in the exact opposite direction. They support me to stop my ideas being carried out.

But to be aware of this conclusion was incompatible with his jovial nature and vague dreams of reform. Before we left him, he wanted to show us his private Kali temple. It was as big as the house and above the doorway floated the mythical Indian swan which cleaves the water without getting wet.

'That's how I want to live in the world,' he said, 'without contact with it.'

*

There is a simple rule of thumb for anyone in a foreign country wanting to get a rough idea of whether a democracy or a dictatorship prevails.

When poor people look as if the first thing they expect from me is a powerful kick in the crotch – then I am in a dictatorship.

*

Sweeping sun in his harsh room – an attic room with windows facing in three directions. He opens them at once and the roar of Bombay city hits the room.

Four spartan rattan chairs round a little table rather like a chafing dish. Rows of books (Laski, Shakespeare, Gita) on the floor below the bare walls. He is a poor man, this socialist and union leader. I know he gratefully accepts second-hand clothing from his better-off bourgeois friends. With his ascetic features and sharp eyes, he makes a strong impression of a clear-sighted, single-minded person.

He describes the situation, calmly and factually.

The number of members of labour organizations is constantly increasing, he says. They are already a power both in the labour market and in society as whole. The legislation drawn up after independence favours the workers. Their standard of living is rising. Racketeers and moneylenders no longer keep them in slavery. Caste differences have been as good as obliterated. The whole country is moving forwards, with industry in the lead.

I sense my confidence rising. Here is a man you have to believe. He is convinced that development is going in the right direction. He knows that everything is being done that can be done.

'Why do the workers live so wretchedly?' I ask. 'Why can't they read? Is the Socialist Party or the trade unions trying to do anything about it?'

'I don't know whether it would be any use to them to be able to read. Most of what is written is rubbish.'

'So you think that in a capitalist society it's better for the workers to remain illiterate?'

'No, that's too extreme. For instance, there are the holy books. One can read them.'

'So religion promotes the development of the workers?'

'Certainly. They have to believe in something when they live so wretchedly.'

'But which religion can help them out of their wretchedness and teach them to see their opportunities?'

'All religions teach faith in the good.'

Sweeping sun in his harsh room. His face is just as intense, his eyes just as clear-sighted as he tells us about religion, which has a powerful reconciling part to play. About development, which must not go too fast. About the generosity and goodwill of factory owners, in which the workers must put their trust. The phrases grow thinner and thinner, more and more marked by impotence. Out of this socialist steps the social mystic. Of his optimism, all that ultimately remains is a nebulous faith that things will be all right in the end – somehow.

Fundamental changes are unnecessary, radical measures inconceivable. And why? Freedom. And what is freedom?

'My home is my castle.'

Silence falls. His idea of freedom remains hovering in the room like a hanging garden – the great lush garden of the Indian upper classes.

I get up. Below the window the city of Bombay spreads out in three directions. If our eyes could penetrate the haze we would see mile after mile of a swampy desert of sacking shacks, slum sheds and dirty seething workers' barracks – dark, barred boxes with a drain in one corner. The coolie-line. Six to eight workers in each hovel. 'My home is my castle.' But those who sleep on stairs and in corridors? Those who share a box on an empty building site? Those who huddle together on the pavement and pull their shirts over their faces?

*

'You are deeply worried, aren't you? Of course you are. All Westerners coming here eventually despair.'

Mr Masani, secretary-general of the largest opposition party in India, invited me to lunch at the Taj Mahal. What shall we have for starters? Prawn cocktail?

We chose the prawns.

'You can be as good a democrat as you like back home,' he went on. 'But India scares you stiff. In panic, you seize on radical means without a thought for the cost in restraint and loss of liberty.'

After two years in China, perhaps I knew something of what they cost. But Mr Masani had already raised his accusing index finger at me and went on, 'That's your situation, isn't it? Don't contradict me. I can always tell.'

I stared in fascination at his ears. One jutted straight out and the other lay flat against his head.

'Half-baked Indian radicals with the government in the lead have the same guilt complex as you have. Out of sheer sentimentality, they want to make the peasants into slaves. Did you know that the government wants to kill all initiative in the rural areas by forbidding the peasants to earn more than three hundred a month?'

No, but I knew that the average income in the rural areas of India was only a tenth of that. And the government has proposed an upper limit not for income but for landownership provisionally expressed in the measure of income. This upper limit is also pure fiction, as the representatives of landowners in the legislative assemblies provide the laws with every possible loophole. But it was already too late for me to object. Mr Masani had marched on.

THE MYTH OF WU TAO-TZU

'This is only the first step,' he continued. 'The government wants to forcibly collectivize the villages. They want to bring in the Chinese system. But we in Swatantra, the Freedom Party, are on the peasant's side. We know he would prefer to be a free man, even if development is going to be slow. The methods that suited you in Europe suit us too. Let them take a hundred years. The peasant doesn't mind waiting. You're the one who is impatient.'

We were just about to tackle the deep-fried fish. It looked delicious – the Taj Mahal is the best hotel in Bombay.

'I can see your objection already,' Masani went on before I had time to open my mouth. 'It's easy for us to sit before a delicious dish and ask the masses to wait, isn't it?'

I nodded, my mouth full.

'You're right. We wouldn't be able to cope with a single day of the kind the peasants will have to live for a hundred years. But that's not the point. You have to learn to differentiate between your problems of conscience and India's social problems. Is it your business or the peasant's? Good. Let the peasant decide. He will choose freedom, however long it takes before he lunches at the Taj Mahal.'

He leaned over the table and for a moment was as stern and intimate as a father.

'I began my political career as a communist,' he said. 'I know what it feels like. It's always unpleasant to eat while others starve. But you simply have to put up with it being unpleasant. Your moral duty is to bear these privileges without ever letting them influence your opinions and actions. It's difficult to do, but possible. I know it. Everyone in this restaurant knows it. Look at us. We're not ashamed.'

I looked at him. He was not ashamed.

65

*

The strange thing was that just as I had succeeded in uprooting my heart, a new little heart started thumping in my ear as I tried to sleep.

True, it was easy to control – I just held my breath. But I couldn't go on holding it forever.

A few days later, another heart started beating behind my right eyelid. I spent all my time holding it in my hand. My eye was trembling like a baby bird.

What should I do?

I once had a heart which pounded for the whole world. But it shrank as I went out into the world, grew as hard as a bullet and became an alien object in my body.

Then it started wandering.

It haunts me everywhere. Sometimes it thumps in my stomach. Sometimes it beats like the tail of a fish slapping my face. Sometimes it races straight through my whole body like an avalanche and I can hardly get up again.

It's my dead heart surging around inside me.

Now I never know where it is. Today it suddenly appeared under my left shoulder blade. Pulsing cautiously at first, with hesitant uneven beats. Then in long series, just as when you roll a marble down a long stairway.

I once had a heart as strong as an oak. But that made no difference. I still had to cut it down. The stump is as hard and dead as a stone.

But all around my body, shoots are already growing.

*

You're a landowner, I suppose?'

The salt crust broke under our feet and we sank into the deep loose sand. This was in Harappa, among the brick ruins left by the 4,000-year-old Indus Valley civilization – an unimagina-tive agricultural and merchant culture which left hardly a single beautiful object behind it, but had good drains, excellent wells, gigantic grain stores and also, in this place, a smelting furnace surrounded by workshops and coolie-lines.

The ground was like a salt-burnt wound, the sun apparently filling the whole sky. We were walking with our hands on our heads, like men disarmed. Prisoners of the sun.

No, I was not a landowner. But the person offering us his umbrella – a sturdily built man in a large turban, followed by one of his 'pupils' – himself owned several thousand acres. The law actually sets a limit of 500 acres. But who hasn't got relat-ives? Who isn't able to draw up a fraudulent contract?

He laughed in a friendly way. He was a very friendly man. We ought not to be out and about in the murderous sun like this. We should sleep at midday in his own bedroom.

The palace-like villa was on a street bearing his own name; in the intimate little dining room there were chairs set out for twenty-four people. The reception room on the ground floor was thirty metres long and furnished with twelve identical sofas upholstered in gold velvet. Opposite the central chandelier hung a huge paint-ing of the Mogul emperor on his throne. The audience room opened up below it, flanked by imitation antique marble busts.

We went in between two wide divans for adjutants and bodyguards, or 'pupils' as our friend called them – silent, sullen youths with powerful lower jaws and crumpled suits. The landowner himself sat in the centre on a gilded throne, behind him the Himalayas modelled in papier mâché.

This is where the peasants come to beg for respite from the rent.

Beyond the pillared halls were suites of empty rooms, the cement in the walls coming through the paint and furnishings. The bedroom was a barracks equipped with South American hotel modernism, the dressing table groaning with sophistic-ated beauty products, the beds with built-in bedside tables and ends like the fronts of American limousines.

But all these objects looked alien in a room where the floor and ceiling shrieked of the primitiveness of the South Asian countryside. And on the inflated beds, very simple and true representatives of their owners, were two ragged and patched, almost homely old quilts.

We crept down.

I lay thinking about this form of society – the realm of the landowner.

They say that the landowner has an economically viable unit of land which must not be divided and frittered away in small parcels. As if the soil were not already cultivated in small bits by poor tenants.

They say the landowner can accumulate capital which the smallholders would eat – but the capital is put into a palace like this and is increased by usury, which in poor countries is the safest and most profitable way of investing money.

They say that the landowner is the only defence against absolute state power. But during the 'democratic' period, our friend's salon was the natural assembly place for the politicians of the district. At the moment, officers are lolling on the gold sofas. As the biggest landowner in the area, he is the town's most powerful man under all regimes.

The peasants are summoned to the stage throne. The 'pupils' are ready, patting their guns meaningfully in their jacket pock-ets. And outside is the salon for the fine gentlemen, the symbol of the owner's social circle and connections, his ability to put society's whole apparatus of power behind his demands.

And all around is the countryside – mile after mile of starved soil and villages beyond despair.

*

That same evening a peasant tried to sell me his daughter at the market in Lahore.

I had gone down to the mosque, to its glimmering cupolas, magical in the dim moonlight, the old city all around. Beneath a thin veil of Eastern seduction – alien dance music, alien scents, rows of open rooms with wall-to-wall mattresses, drums, girls showing their arts – here you look into the sexual and economic realities of a stagnant society.

Excitable gangs, ready for violence, roam drunkenly through streets seething with police. You can buy very lifelike large dolls resembling a three-year-old girl in lacy underwear.

In a free society, all tastes are provided for. Little girls dance and sing for you before you satisfy yourself with them. The eager little children with their clear voices are touching as they imitate the movements of an adult woman. They are offered quite naturally, in lighted rooms open to the street. Children become slightly less of a burden if in their early years they learn to contribute to the upkeep of the family.

The peasants are driven into town by their poverty, their oxen waiting by the mosque. The men go and stand in the market square, their faces as yet unused and filled with dark intent.

He was very serious as he offered me sexual intercourse with his little girl as he held her in his arms.

*

When you leave the Indian subcontinent and drive up through the Khyber Pass which connects Pakistan to Afghanistan, you see armed peasants for the first time. You meet them everywhere along the roads and out in the villages, their rifles on their backs.

Afghanistan – an old tribal society where man is still not

subdued. Everyone I meet considers himself to be just as much a human being as I am. After India, this is wonderful, refreshing, an almost unbelievable experience.

Is it their religion? Or is it the mountains? Or that they have never been colonized? It is certainly not a high standard of living and modern civilization. The poverty is profound. Here as everywhere the big farmer, the usurer and the merchant form a steadfast trinity. But there is a counterbalance.

'The rich have traditional duties to the village and the family. That has an economically levelling effect.'

'Those who have power usually know how to circumvent duties of that kind,' I say.

His amused eyes glitter.

'Nothing would suit them better. But it would not be safe.'

We had come to talk about fruit-growing there in the district. The apples cost a few pence a bushel but are sold in Kabul for a pound. The difference goes to the merchant and his truck. The growers have now formed an association and are going to buy a truck and sell their apples themselves.

'What do you do when the merchant's "pupils" pour water into the petrol?' I ask. 'When you have your windscreen secretly smashed, your tyres slashed and your engine keeps stopping? As usually happens to the co-op's truck when the mark-up is threatened?'

'The merchants are not very pleased,' says the Afghan. 'Naturally not. But it wouldn't be wise for them to try anything on the truck.'

He was the head of the agricultural school and did not carry a rifle. But he knew the peasants did.

It is said that a travelling foreigner can get shot in Afghanistan. No such risk in India, but I would rather be afraid myself than see others cringe.

The British brought peace and order to India. They created a kind of rule of law, but that also entailed the right of the landowner, the usurer and the merchant to oppress. It made the masses helpless in the hands of those who had the economic and social advantage.

Guns and a wild determination to use them were what saved the Afghans from being civilized by the British Empire. And nothing but guns and determination will, in a pre-democratic, pre-organized society, guarantee that the interests of the people are to some extent satisfied.

I am a pacifist. But after seeing the fear, the mad fright in Indian eyes, that unnatural abasement both ostentatious and ashamed, but most of all cowed, humiliated and broken – after having been in India, I am glad to see armed peasants.

*

Deserts.

Miles and miles of slopes disappearing into a soft haze, the earth rising like a mist round the mountains, their peaks clearly outlined in the chilly air.

Great flocks of sheep live off the invisible desert plants – a few hours after they have disappeared a fresh, almost spicy, sourish scent strikes you from the sand where they have been grazing.

Oases – bouquets of poplar in clay vessels – surrounded by fields irrigated by *kanat*. The vegetation appears to have been dropped from the surrounding mountains, running down the slopes and accumulating like water at the bottom of the hollow: an even, thick, deep patch of almost green-black corn.

This is where the villages are, crowded together like honeycombs, the houses composed of clay cells covered with cupolas. Neat little dwellings, no dirt or flies, as if sterilized by the desert wind. You step into them from the heat and the searing light out in the sand as if into a cool sauna: the chilly darkness inside is as great a relief as fire is to the frozen.

But the houses are empty, recently abandoned. In the greatest of haste.

The army post on the road is on full alert, tanks brought up, machine guns manned, everyone gathered round a spot on the road – an even, thick, deep patch of almost black blood.

There has been a peasants' revolt in Fars.

The mansion of the village owner looms above the oasis, a fortress tower surrounded by a dense, flourishing garden. His power rests on his control of the irrigation system – the *kanat* underground aqueducts – which creates this magical circle of life in the sand.

Up on the surface you can see them for kilometres like series of molehills. They resemble huge footprints leading to the patch on the road.

Oases – a drop of life pressed out of desert and death. Power and wealth – a drop of death pressed out of others' lives.

4

We came home today.

The table is there.

The flames in the pine. Like fire, like the lake water.

Year streaks on the surface: dark winters and light summers.

All Sweden. All my former self.

This is what I wanted: clean wood.

A surface continuing inwards.

A material living in death.

A hope that truth can be united with joy.

*

Must find the connection with this past self.

But it is like going into a nursery and finding your old toys scattered all over the floor.

This centre that I started out from and to which I must now learn to return. A meeting place between inner and outer worlds.

Ruysbroek the mystic and Ruysbroek the traveller, for a long time I thought they were the same person.

I very much wanted to be that man.

Proust. In him, life is not just a road which we go along. On the contrary, our experiences form a kind of body.

Our lives *are* ourselves. We *are* our lives.

It is a matter of keeping hold of these experiences, this body of life, and not letting them float away and vanish.

Losing your memory is losing your self. Losing a memory is

losing a part of your self. Holding on to your experiences, with the whole force of your memory assembling your life and holding it close to you, is to preserve your very self.

Man's most important task, according to Proust. In the actual recalling, he thought he had found a paradise in which insight can be united with rapture.

Truth with joy.

But it is not the spring that makes the water.

A spring – only a place where the water manages to emerge which in the depths is to be found everywhere.

Black water yesterday.

Taste of blood today.

*

In Proust: his viewpoint is predetermined, he knows where he wants to take me.

In Hesse: his viewpoint has suddenly shifted, the matter driven to its extreme and turning there.

In Musil: I participate in an experiment, the novel feels its way through unknown territory.

Proust is on his way towards an anticipated disillusion, which Musil starts out from and tries to overcome.

'He who has not seen the struggle in my work has not seen its thoroughness either,' said Musil, when comparing himself to Proust. His satire – a way of sterilizing instruments before the operation.

Proust takes the past by surprise.

Musil penetrates into what is to come.

Hesse has meant most to me.

The Glass Bead Game. Is the episode with the scent of elder aimed at Proust?

Hesse: not life but culture is body. What he wishes to keep 'close to him' is tradition.

These two works are profoundly antagonistic.

Proust reproduces the past in the present.

Hesse projects past and present on to the future.

Musil projects present and future on to the past. The future forces its way into his work with all the strength of a past.

The present in Musil?

The beating heart in a great hovering bird with one wing in the past, the other in what is to come.

Musil in the garden. Hesse in the garden.

Two German writers in exile. Only a few miles between them. Kakania – Castalia.

Hesse on *The Man Without Qualities* in 1931 and 1933: he praises the great artistry, which 'gives substance and even warmth to the somewhat glassy world of the novel'. Did he see the connection?

The introduction of *The Glass Bead Game* was published the following year. The answer to Musil's suggestion of a secretariat for spiritual exactness?

Both have this 'sense of hitherto unborn realities'. Both tried to create a spiritual existence which could balance the world.

I read them to re-establish contact with myself as tradition. To regain what I have lost – that feeling of meaning and justification tradition once provided.

Disappearance as a motif in Musil, Hesse, Proust. It is the myth of Wu Tao-tzu stepping into the work of art.

Osvald Sirén, in his history of Chinese art, mentions the myth of Wu Tao-tzu but only in passing. I can't find it in Chinese handbooks.

Why did he disappear? What company did he leave behind? Did he experience the culture of his day as desperate, meaningless?

Or was it an act of artistic self-confidence? An attempt to verify art in life?

What is attractive in the myth: the courage to solitude.

The courage to disappear and continue alone on the other side of what is visible in art.

*

I would like to write a book about Wu Tao-tzu using Jack London's method in *The People of the Abyss*. That was one of the first 'real' books I read as a boy, the words now charged with memories as I read it again.

His experiment has always fascinated me. It contains my own story. But I repeated it in a different direction, using different material.

A book on where Wu Tao-tzu went after the gates had opened.

I can see it now. Literature has been really meaningful for me only as Utopia. In my books, and not only there but also in the hopes I have, in my demands on life, in the motives for my actions, briefly – everywhere it may have practical consequences, I discover the same presumptions as in Hesse, in Musil, in Proust, as in the whole line of writers who have shaped me: that man can step into art.

The opposite of the East End is not the West End. But where is it, then? I want to know how people are living there and what they are living for. In short, I want to live there myself.

'Live there yourself!' said people with the most disapproving expressions. 'You can't, you know.'

It must be possible. The prospect of a clearer and freer way of

living has always been held out to me. It must exist. I've seen it
in poetry and pictures. I've heard it in music. There's a
fearlessness there which makes my life foolish. There are
opportunities for happiness there which frighten me more than
unhappiness. There's an abyss in reverse, and one falls upwards.

Why, then, do I live as I do?

Not even the professors at the university – scholarly men
and women who without a moment's hesitation would have
sent me to the darkest corners of the archives and the innermost petty details of the bibliographies – not even they could
help me.

'Art as a way of living?'

'Yes, of course. An excellent subject for a study of motifs.'

'As a personal experiment?'

'What do you mean?'

'To examine the habitability of poetry. To live in a work of art.'

'Like inhabiting a house? You can't.'

'To test the ways of the spirit in practice.'

'That's – hmm – unprecedented. I don't think we can do
anything for you.'

Clearly I had to manage on my own. Having burnt my boats,
I was now free to enter a world of which no one seemed to know
anything. Like Jack London in the summer of 1902 in the city of
the same name. But in the opposite direction. He stepped out of
fiction, I wanted to enter. I wanted to be present where culture
was being enacted – an observer in disguise, an eyewitness of the
spirit on the lookout for a better life than ours.

*

I found the best directions in Hesse.

In the summer of 1956, newly married, we lived in Harry
Järv's apartment in Solberga and I read *The Glass Bead Game*

for the first time. I had been reviewing travel books for three years and had begun to understand that my image of the world was the result of a systematic distortion with commercial intentions. I was working on a book on advertising.

The Glass Bead Game did not suit me. I found the same touching immaturity as in *Steppenwolf*, but without the naked-ness of pain, with no desperation – instead a kind of pretentious pomposity. The novel contained everything I detest: anti-sen-suality, elitism resulting in a seminary of ambitious careerists, a veneer, official airs, spiritual bureaucracy (even Prussianism, res-idence permits, passes), an air of pastiche and irony, Hegelian dialectics, Spenglerian music of doom, a vapid 'magnanimity', worship of nobility, flirtation with the Church, a snobbish dis-dain for the contemporary and most of all a tone, that delicate tone of being slightly grander, slightly superior ...

And yet hardly a day went by without my thinking about the book. Particularly in the spring of 1957, when I was panned in all the newspapers for the book on advertising and we played Bach and Vivaldi all day. *The Glass Bead Game* was the only book that could suck the poison out of the snake-bite of the day. I went back to the roots of the motif, read *Hours in the Garden* and admired its Arcadian revolt against the consumerism all round me, that sublime sabotage of the occupation of the age. What did it matter to me that others talked about 'the difference between a glass bead game and genuine art'? The words were taken as a symbol of formal perfection without content and expression, a meaningless game with no beating heart, no visionary force, an empty game with false and glittering pearls.

To me it was something else.

I was particularly interested in the complicated time struc-ture in the novel. A time which really lies behind ours is regarded as a past, starting from, for us, a future point in time.

The explanation is simple. The nineteenth century's judgement of our time interests no one. It is like listening to a poor relation from the country. But let the year 2400 pronounce the same judgement – then it's the voice of a superior speaking! Hesse exploits this superstitious respect for the future to build up Castalia as a Utopia. When the criticism starts biting, when even the year 2400 turns out to be subject to the failings and threats of the present and to be threatened by present dangers, then our prejudices of time have been broken down. The future has lost its prestige. The past has lost its stigma. What is left is a sense of timelessness, of a *now* which has always occurred and always will.

I let myself disappear into that now. Disappear into that perfectly balanced aquarium, into that artistic *perpetuum mobile*, into that smooth round ball of sheer light reflecting itself. A globe with neither entrance nor exit, with no living human beings, no smell or taste. Where all colours are extinguished in white. An old man's work of seductive brilliance, perhaps even a value dream which with force and endurance assembles all the great cultures into the same human focal point. But can that dream be realized?

That was what I wanted to know.

I have loved it. It is the promise I have loved, the immense promise of an inner room common to arts and sciences into which, through exercises and ecstasies, one could make one's way. Goethe said, '*Meine Bildung hat sich gesteigert.*' ('My education has been heightened.') He meant an intensified humanity. And enclosed in that inner infinite room, human beings would finally become human.

*

I discovered the connection with Paul Klee. *The Thinking Eye*. The picture as an analysis of concepts.

Spengler on the music of Bach as mathematical analysis.

The formulae of the glass bead game as a kind of Gödel numbering of the spirit.

Keyser's metaphorical application of group theory in *Mathematical Philosophy*.

An Indian raga begins so that it can be danced. I experience it as body in movement. As the pace slowly increases and imperceptibly steps over the border of what can be danced, nonetheless the sense of body is retained, and the music appears to testify to tremendous possibilities for movement never before imagined.

Language begins so that it can be practised. I experience it as reality and action. As the pace slowly increases and imperceptibly steps over the border of what can be practised, nonetheless the sense of reality is retained, and the language appears to testify to tremendous possibilities for action never before imagined.

To Poincaré, mathematics is more an art than a science. Some combinations are more 'beautiful, serious, important' than others. Solutions can be called 'classic' or 'baroque', and the work of the great mathematicians can be identified by their distinctive personal character.

Like the mathematician, the artist works with a system of symbols which makes no statement about reality. But it is only because reality can be interpreted and understood in terms of these systems that they are meaningful to us.

Just as there is a literature of chess in which the movements of the pieces are credited with a meaning, in which the game regarded as calculus has an 'interpretation', I tried to interpret *The Glass Bead Game.*

*

Autumn 1958.

> Billiards was his favourite game, and he was not only a
> master of it, but he also used to be particularly lively, happy
> and witty during the game. He often used to give the three
> balls the names of people from our circle of acquaintances
> and then construct from the different positions of the balls
> whole novels full of foolish and caricatured comparisons. In
> that way, he played calmly, lightly and elegantly throughout,
> so that it was a joy to watch him.

I took this passage in Hesse's novel *Peter Camenzind* as my
starting point for a book on *The Glass Bead Game*. The novel
was to be regarded as a game in which the characters are accu-
mulators rather than people, in which the action in the novel
is used as a way of providing order between concepts – the
ideogrammatical method.

Studied Pound's *Guide to Kulchur* and followed the tracks to
Fenollosa. Realized I had to learn some Chinese to understand
the glass bead game. It became a passion. Karlgren's *Grammata
Serica* became my artistic bible. There, in the principle by
which the Chinese language forms characters, I at last found a
possible way of expressing things previously closed to me.

Now I don't know any longer. The experience of how characters were formed is not as clearly demarcated as at first. It
has become perfectly natural to me.

I went to China.

At Peking University, Father Jacobus lectured on the impor-
tance of the slave trade to the industrialization of Europe. On
'the financial drain' in India. On the 4 May movement as a
rebellion against Castalia. The Long March – Knecht's flight.

Plinio Designori arrived on the Castalian coast with only thirty men. During the march into Havana, he met the friend of his youth, Joseph Knecht. Their conversation did not work out as Hesse had thought. It is said that Knecht has gone underground to lead the guerrillas in South America.

Who really was Joseph Knecht?

Tolstoy died at the home of the stationmaster in Astapovo.

Wittgenstein put the philosophers of Europe to work for the next hundred years. Inspired by Tolstoy's teachings, he then gave away his fortune and became a primary school teacher in the Austrian Alps.

Was it Knecht who was murdered by Stalin's agents in Mexico on 20 August 1940? Or did his plane crash in Africa in 1961?

I know that Bertrand Russell travelled round China in the 1920s giving lectures on the non-violent road to socialism. Mao Tse-tung heard him in Changsha. Over two-thirds of the population of the world live in misery, he wrote to Chou in France. Without violence, it will take a hundred years before they are liberated. 'How can we bear that?'

Mao found no reason to change his mind.

On the other hand, Russell did.

During the Cuban Missile Crisis, I sat fairly still in my room in Peking. Herman Kahn led the game. When the end was near, Goethe and Father Sosima came to see the old Music Master. They died together. Even Goethe stank.

*

Is there an art more important than the world?

That is the question the story of Joseph Knecht finally asks.

On the wall of his cell, Hesse painted a landscape containing everything that had given him joy in life. Mountains and rivers. Seas and clouds. Widespread forests. In the same way, the glass bead game concentrates all the possibilities of the spirit into one single point. Knecht is the most elevated player of the game. In his figure, the question is brought to a head.

In all his writing, Hesse has taken it upon himself to answer the question in the affirmative. That is a very difficult venture which stretches all his powers. Not until it is almost too late does he discover what he is about to succeed in doing.

Is it the function of art to make mass graves banal? Is it the task of thought to make starvation uninteresting? Spiritual happiness that makes the world irrelevant will also make suffering, oppression and extermination irrelevant.

At the very moment victory is within reach, Hesse finds he has been fighting on the wrong side. This point is the peripeteia of his writing. All his life, in disguise after disguise, he has sought to leave the world and step into art, and now, as he is finally on the point of succeeding, he sends his last character back into the world.

*

On television last night. A programme on the care of the mentally ill.

The old exercise yard at Långbro mental hospital was shown. The walls had been pulled down. But the inmates still don't go out. They stay inside the wall that once existed.

And I?

Perhaps at one period in your life you have to tie up the sack from within. That's necessary to create a self into which to disappear. There is no world without self.

Don't participate! Refuse! That was my imperative. I refused to admit the contemporaneity in the present to which we are all subordinated. I wanted to reach the contemporaneity in art which is independent of the day. I locked myself in. And in there I built the catapult that was to hurl me out into the world.

Now I realize my dependency. I am a product of forces beyond myself. If man is to be changed, then those forces must be changed. There is no self without world.

*

What was it that happened in India?

I seriously began to doubt my own judgement as well as that of all my contemporaries.

I grew contemptuous of my innermost strivings.

I realized that my reason functioned within the framework of an insanity which invalidated it.

In its advertisements, the Indian state promises a piece of genuine Indian rope to everyone who comes to the greatest democracy in the world, to the country of temples and tigers. It's a realistic advertisement. What everyone who goes there needs more than anything else is a piece of genuine Indian rope.

But if you don't hang yourself in your hotel room on the very first evening – and what use would that be? – then a creeping dehumanization occurs. The simplest humanity demands that you try to save the life of another person. In a city where the cleansing department collects the bodies of the dead off the streets at dawn and in uncertain cases turns the sleeping over with a foot to see if they are still alive – in a city of that kind, even the simplest humanity demands too much. You lose faith in it.

It was in such a city 'I' disappeared. In the bed where 'I' had lain, there was still someone who, without noticeable discomfort, heard another human being shaking with cold on the stone floor outside the door. In 'my' place, someone went on living and eating and winding up the car window when a leper thrust his stumps in. Someone who, day after day, year after year, rationally satisfies his own needs. Who has given up hope of 'himself' and accepted this rationality within its framework of insanity.

*

The swan of Indian myth which cleaves the water without getting wet.

Is that me?

Our nails whitened, bruises wandered over our bodies, hair loosened and fell out. Stroking your wife's head and receiving a handful of loose hair. Every day we swept up our hair off the floor. It was not just a shortage of food but a physical symptom of an ideological crisis, the body's answer to the Chinese judgement of us and our part of the world. Oppressors. Bloodsuckers!

It was possible to grow up with a very good conscience in the Sweden of my youth, already through the awareness of intellectually being in control of the situation. That gave you a great sense of security. And at the same time, quite gratis, you could call yourself a champion of justice and humanity. I thought the question was whether from these prerequisites I would be able to accept China. It became China that rejected me and my prerequisites.

Yet China was a calming experience. The responsibility was no longer ours, as the country belonged to the other, the communist, side. I saw China's successes as a result of a Europeanization. Oppression and conformity as a lack of democracy. Suffering, starvation as a consequence of ideological mistakes. The Party admitted these mistakes and tried to overcome them. The Russians had already renounced their Stalinism.

Maoism was more benign from the start. Everything appeared to be in order.

But these defence mechanisms did not work in India. I saw that the image of the world I had built up in China was false. It was not true that democracy offered a more humane route to progress. Suffering and oppression were still more tangible in India. The country was heading for disaster. And democracy was nothing but a veil thrown over the realities of power in a class society.

'They support me to stop my ideas being carried out.'

I had not had the strength to make myself aware of that conclusion. The swan of myth was gliding above my door too – the dream of cleaving the water without getting wet.

I had always had my suspicions. I occasionally went into attack. But I belonged to the loyal opposition, which in the end always votes for full and thankful freedom of responsibility for the committee.

With every word I wrote, I stood surety for a world in which everyone, with a little effort, could become a decent human being.

In India, all that fell apart. I discarded that commitment. All ambitions to see the world in that way are impossible and faulty. They can be maintained only in garden environments. Confronted with reality, they result in moral collapse, in a mixture of cynicism and rage.

*

In her book *Eichmann in Jerusalem: A Report on the Banality of Evil* (1963), Hannah Arendt states that before they began the extermination of the Jews, the Nazis were uncertain whether it would be possible to carry out from a purely practical point of view. Would they be able to get the Jews to walk on their own two feet to their doom, each with a small suitcase, in the middle of the night and with no prior notification? How would their neighbours react when they found the empty apartments in the morning?

Two experiments were carried out to investigate the matter.

The first concerned the deportation of 1,300 Jews from Stettin, carried out in one single night on 13 February 1940, the very first deportation of German Jews. Heydrich had ordered it on the grounds that 'their apartments were urgently needed for reasons connected with the war effort'. The Jews were taken to the Lublin area under atrocious conditions.

The second deportation took place in the autumn of the same year, when all the Jews in Baden and Saarpfalz – about 7,500 men, women and children – were taken away.

It is odd to think that these 8,800 people, defenceless against an utterly superior power, presumably just by smashing windows, kicking, biting and refusing to move, might have saved millions of their own race. It is even odder to think that by being upset and asking awkward questions their neighbours might have been able to achieve the same result.

But the experiment succeeded. The Jews meekly went. Their neighbours said nothing.

When you see the gaping social chasms between the countries of the world, when you witness the arrogance of the rich and the wretchedness of the poor, you ask yourself why nothing happens. Why does nothing happen? People tolerate starvation, ignorance and contempt. Their friends die of diseases that could be cured. Their children die. They go on working as before. They lose their jobs. But they go on all the same, meekly and uncomplaining, to their own destruction. Day after day. Year after year.

There is no need to drag away the poor of the world to be

gassed. They go by themselves, on their own feet to annihilation, in the middle of the day and with no prior notification. And their neighbours say nothing.

*

He who says nothing. He consents
He who whispers. He lies.
He who screams. He goes unheard.

*

It is sometimes said that reason and humanity have no place in the world of today. I cannot share this dark view. Humanity has a task in our day as well.

On Christmas Eve 1966, the International Red Cross announced that South Vietnam had requested immediate aid with food, clothes and medical supplies for 1.5 million refugees.

This request ought not to have surprised anyone. The refugees the Red Cross were appealing for were victims of a conscious, intentional and consistently pursued American policy which had been known about since it was introduced in 1965.

It had turned out that a resistance movement which had the rural population on its side was difficult if not impossible to defeat. The guerrillas moved like fish in the waters of the people's sea. So all the 'water' had to be emptied out. The guerrillas had to be deprived of their supporting population. The USA had to try to transfer the population from the areas controlled by the NFL to other, government-controlled, areas. In 1.5 million cases, it had been successful.

The strategic bombing started to work on this removal of population on 19 February 1965, ground-strafing aircraft from a series of bases in South Vietnam and Thailand taking part. Rocket-firing helicopters and planes spraying chemicals were involved in the same mission, backed by artillery and infantry. The result, attested by the International Red Cross, was 1.5 million refugees in need of immediate help.

When this policy was introduced and while it was being enforced, a chorus of voices all over the world appealed to the USA to stop. We appealed in the name of reason and humanity. The USA was not deterred, not even when the Secretary-General of the United Nations or the World Council of Churches was speaking. Relying on military power and its enormous propaganda resources, the USA mercilessly implemented the policy decided upon.

But then, when the hideous results of this policy began to be seen, now the time had come to turn to the humanitarian institutions and beg for help. That was the right place for humanity. Compassionate people all over the world could then join in and deal with supplies for 1.5 million victims.

It might perhaps be supposed that the rich and powerful USA could surely afford to look after the refugees as they came pouring out of the bombed territories. But we should not demand the impossible. Even before they arrived, these people had been very expensive for the USA. Bombing their villages, burning their homes, blowing up their houseboats, poisoning their fields, maiming their children and killing their parents had cost the USA tremendous sums – according to conservative estimates, at least $100,000 per dead guerrilla. It could hardly be expected of the USA that it should also be able to look after the survivors. No, it was more appropriate in this case for the International Red Cross to take over.

Humanity has a task in our day as well. I fear that this task will only grow in the years ahead of us.

*

'During my journey in South Africa, I asked everyone capable of discussing, not just making propaganda, how they saw the future. Many of them, within different camps, believed in a disaster, a race war, whether in the form of revolution or genocide, a bloody defeat for the whites. Those who didn't believe that reckoned on concessions before it was too late, with an activating of the peaceful campaign for reform (possibly in the form of strikes and passive resistance) which would enable the whites successively to soften their rule and finally accept equality. No one can judge whether that possibility exists or where a development in that direction would lead. But one thing I think is certain: as things are at the moment, white domination cannot last long. Perhaps there is no solution, in our humanitarian and optimistic sense; if there is one, it will be through the whites meeting the oppressed halfway, in a rebirth of the ideas which have so long been said to justify white domination.'

Herbert Tingsten, 1954

*

Can social and economic liberation be achieved without violence?

I shall try to answer the question. But first let me ask one myself.

Artur Lundkvist has been asked to declare how many years of war he considers a revolution in India to be worth.

That's a reasonable request.

But should we not in the same way be prepared to state exactly what sacrifices we consider our present society to be worth?

We belong to an economic system.

Perhaps it is inescapable that the system has to tolerate a certain number of starving and dead. Just as we tolerate a certain amount of unemployment.

But at 50 per cent unemployment, we would have long since reached the conclusion that our form of society is not capable of carrying out its tasks.

Is there a tolerance point for world need? How many millions of starving people for how many years?

Starvation, it could be objected, is relative.

But when starvation becomes death, it is absolute. An absolute limit there.

I can accept a system that demands a million (10 million, 100 million) casualties – but then the limit is reached, and I would consider a higher figure unacceptable.

Causes of death are often difficult to establish.

Some die of disease, others of great age, forty years or so.

A direct relation between misery and death is often hard to prove.

But when wretchedness leads to rebellion and the most powerful representatives of the economic system intervene with bombs and napalm to quell the disturbances – then there is a direct relation between system and sacrifice.

It ought to be possible to set a definite limit. How many millions?

Causes of rebellion, it could be objected, are also hard to establish.

Revolution can be blamed on subversion or infiltration.

The number of victims in suppressing the rebellion is not a reasonable measure.

I have suggested three ways of measuring the number of sacrifices we are willing to accept in order to keep our present economic system. We could measure the number of starving, the number of premature deaths or the number of casualties when the misery produces rebellion.

None of these measures is free of objections.

Only a preliminary attempt to fix the breaking point.

It ought to be an urgent task of research to find better criteria.

Which allow us to calculate exactly the price we are willing to let other people pay.

To be able to keep an economic system favourable to ourselves.

Can liberation be achieved without violence?

By 'liberation' I mean liberation from this economic system.

From the present way of sharing natural resources, results of production and freedom.

The system is established with violence.

It has always exercised violence.

Seeing your children starve while your rulers live in affluence and sell the country to foreigners.

To be kept down in ignorance and degradation.

Dying of diseases which could have been cured.

That is being exposed to violence.

The power of large landowners over their landless workers.
   The iron grip of feudal family systems on the individual.
   The exploitation by moneylenders and slum owners of their victims.
   The encroachment of foreign capital interests on the sovereignty of a poor country.
   All these are forms of violence and oppression.

Can it be brought down without violence?
   That depends on us.
   For it is we, the Western nations, who are the upholders and profiteers of the economic system.
   Our task is to stop ourselves.

Can anyone stop himself?
   The whites couldn't in South Africa.
   The land barons couldn't in South America.
   The USA couldn't in South Vietnam.
   It is impossible as long as we are kept in an illusory world.

Germany after the 1945 collapse.
   The first of the world I saw with my own eyes.
   No adult I knew had been outside the borders of Sweden.
   The train went slowly through Germany. Slowly and hesitantly. Searching for the rails amid the wreckage.
   Took two days then.
   You had time to see every face.
   Apathetic, ruined, shattered.

Distorted steel skeletons, stunted churches, obliterated towns.

Landscape of ruins. Destruction in which every heap of rubble was a mass grave.

Cripples and cellar people.

Hungry children running shouting along the track, their hands outstretched.

Along the international train which slowly, slowly bored its way through the heart of Europe.

Sights which branded themselves on me.

Sights which made me a pacifist.

Since then, arms technology has advanced.

The six years of the Second World War can now be concentrated into six minutes.

And repeated once a day for six months without emptying the stores of armaments.

This threat still hangs over mankind.

We got used to it.

After five or ten years, Germany was back on her feet.

The images of need were obliterated. Europe was moving ahead.

Marshall Aid.

Colonies.

In which exports to the USA during the critical years increased by hundreds, sometimes thousands of percentage points and supplied Europe with currency.

It was not called 'development loan'. But Europe revived and flourished.

That was when they started talking about 'underdeveloped countries'.

It would perhaps take a little longer there.
But it would work. We all thought so.
The matter was regarded as a technical problem.
Or a kind of international social service.

During the 1960s it turned out:
1) That things were going the wrong way.
   The gaps were widening, debts increasing.
   The poor in the poor countries became even poorer.
   It turned out that the problems were just as political as
      they were economic.
   The privileged strata gained from stagnation.
   They were economically and politically allied to us.
   They had our support.
   And would go on having it even more as the tensions
      between rich and poor intensified.
   Who dares believe that opinion will mature in time?
   In Europe? In the USA?
   We will stay on the side of the privileged in order to
      maintain our own privileges.

It also turned out:
2) That national freedom seldom brings with it economic
   freedom.
   Anti-colonialism itself once provided hope.
   When the peoples became free, then their economic and
      social problems would also be solved.
   But it turned out that our lead was too great.
   The liberated countries have been kept in economic
      dependence.

During our industrialization we had opportunities they
    have not.
We were able to move our surplus population to three
    continents and parts of a fourth.
Plundering, slave trade and ruthless exploitation of
    workers created capital.
Which secured cheap raw materials and protected markets
    in the colonies.
The developing countries cannot repeat this.

They gave us an immense 'loan' for our development.
    It was now being demanded back with compound interest.
    But according to our calculations, they are in debt to us.
    A debt that steadily increases.

The resources put into armaments and surplus consumption
could have saved the world.
    Today that would hardly work.
    Tomorrow that will be impossible.
    And, as yet, that is not 'realistic politics' anywhere.
    We will go on as before.
    Exploiting our economic and military superiority.
    Taking more than we give.
    Using the little we give to increase our opportunities for
taking even more.

It also turned out:
3) That equality on our level has become impossible.
    Simply because natural resources are insufficient.
    Even if the absolutely incredible happened.

Even if we stopped supporting the ruling privileged.
Even if we were to think again. Begin to repay on a
   gigantic scale the unjust gains of the past.
In golden harmony between wolves and lambs.
The world cannot live at our level.

Our consumption of oil, coal, paper, metal, meat etc. cannot be
multiplied by the population of the world.
   Synthetic materials?
   They entail changing raw materials.
   Not that one can dispense with raw materials.

It is not a question of time and sacrifice before the billions of
six continents have a car and a house.
   That can never happen.
   Natural resources would come to an end in a few decades, in
some cases months.

We have got used to a standard.
   We regard it as our right.
   It's not just a taunt to the world today.
   It always will be.
   We must be alone in that. Forever.
   We have created a lifestyle which makes injustice perman-
ent and inescapable.

Is the conclusion clear?
   We have to become poor again.
   Or uphold our privileges with violence.
   No people, even less a continent, has yet voluntarily chosen
poverty.
   Nor are there any prospects of us being about to.

It also turned out:
4) That technological development does not only mean
   mechanized agriculture with many times larger harvests,
   new sources of energy through nuclear power etc.
   It also creates frightening social prospects.

The population explosion happens at the same time as the automation breakthrough.

The Western peoples obtained a say in government during a period when workers were needed in production.
   That period has gone.
   The peoples of the Third World are demanding the same thing just when their opportunities for peaceful influence have become almost non-existent.

The technically natural thing to do now is to industrialize a country with methods which scarcely affect the general population.
   For humanitarian reasons alone, factories are occasionally built to 'create employment'.
   How long will such reasons be allowed to stop true technological development?

To be able to compete within our system, the developing countries have to use our technology.
   It was not created to provide employment.
   On the contrary.
   The world's proletariat is on its way to becoming superfluous.
   Large parts are already nothing but a burden.
   For the small high-producing and high-consuming groups whose leaders rule the world.

The economically optimal population of India is no more than a third, perhaps only a tenth of the present population.

No need for prudery here.

Modern weapons have taught us to think straight into the unthinkable.

Tell me what will happen.

When once the majority of humanity have become techno-logically surplus and incapable of supporting themselves on our terms.

At the same time rebellious with hunger and economically unimportant.

What will then stop a final solution of the world problem?

You suddenly feel powerless.

Strange. You were part of the decision-making.

On where alcohol is permitted to be served.

Strange, this feeling of total, annihilating powerlessness – in the only part of the world where free people are in power.

Is social and economic liberation possible without violence?

The question appears to presume that it is possible *with* violence.

I don't think so.

Vietnam provided illusions.

But Vietnam fought against the paper tiger under the pro-tection of world opinion.

Nothing is more unreliable.

Where will this opinion stand when the extent of the dis-aster becomes evident?

Vietnam fought under the protection of the bombs of the Soviet Union.

Nothing is more unreliable.

Russia would hardly expose herself to mass destruction to stop the mass destruction of others.

The wealthy white countries are so utterly superior to the poor countries of the world.

Modern arms are so effective.

That no insurmountable difficulties need arise.

Vietnam was a clumsy war.

It cost American lives and American prestige.

It will certainly not be repeated – not in that way.

Out of consideration for opinion, cruel and ineffectual means were used.

Napalm. Rockets. Defoliants. Etc.

But naturally the USA had arms which could have settled the Vietnam War in a few hours, if it had been politically possible to use them.

I think it will be politically possible.

It would be an illusion to believe in remorse and renewal.

What we can expect are aggression, racism, fascism.

The terror the darkening world situation is creating will not lead to penance and redress.

It will prepare the way for leaders with radical final solutions.

Those who enforced white supremacy – Vorster, Ian Smith, Wallace and Goldwater and their kind – all bide their time.

They recognize an overture when they hear one.

They were no night birds from a dim past that had lost their way in the daylight of our time.

We are the ones who have not noticed the twilight beginning to descend around us.

As early as in the 1930s, there was a man who had the nerve to demand '*Lebensraum*' for his people and his race.

How much has the population of the world grown since then?

How many poor and starving do you think the world can bear before our leaders rediscover that word?

When I was editing Ekelund's diary, I searched for a long time for an explanation of the note on 13 December 1913: 'The Herero blacks swear by their mothers' tears.'

It turned out that the Herero were a people in south-west Africa whose population, from 1904 to 1907, was decimated by the Germans from 80,000 to 15,000. It cost £30 million. It would be cheaper today. Tomorrow it will cost almost nothing. By 1913 the German colony was operating at a profit.

The governor's name was Göring. His son was one of those responsible for the extermination of the Jews in Europe.

What had been done by the thousand was repeated by the million.

Even that will turn out to be insufficient.

What has been done in millions will be repeated in billions.

I shall now try to answer the question you have asked me. Is social and economic liberation possible without violence?

No.
Is it possible with violence?
No.

*

I was born at the end of the New Age, just before the Dark Ages began to return.

I had a wife, an apartment, food and books. I was considered an amiable writer and lived at peace with the world. I travelled in Europe and America. Everything seemed to be in order.

Then I went to China.

My education began. India and Vietnam continued it. I was thrown into studies which provided despair without end.

My friends are perhaps right when they say that ever since then my writing has lost its beauty and harmony. What are beauty and harmony when you are running for dear life between crumbling walls? I am beginning to believe that all my artistic endeavours have been a mistake. My task, that personal probing ahead I once called my mission, no longer exists.

That is where I am today. But the past often fills me more than the present, nor can I clearly separate what is to come from what has already been. I live very much in the future. So I need not end my autobiography here, but will calmly continue.

I spent a few years in Latin America. My reports from there gained approval for their exemplary objectivity. At the same time, it was said, they constituted 'a flaming appeal, impossible to neglect'. But no one any longer seriously believed that the catastrophe could be prevented. It became increasingly clear that a greater awareness of the world does not lay foundations for a new solidarity, but rather arouses feelings of terror and guilt which favour reaction.

The brief period when democratic freedoms could be used for attacking established society had already gone. Far too great economic interests were at stake. When it became clear that 'democracy' would mean a steeply reduced standard of living under a world government in which hostile peoples of other races had decisive influence, that ideology was abandoned as obsolete.

The apparently long-gone nationalism in Europe arose again with tremendous force as a response to the nationalism of the oppressed peoples. As the economic gaps fell largely along racial lines, white people closed ranks to defend their privileges.

A new technology for mass-sterilization through drinking water and spraying from the air provided great but short-lived hopes. Then other thoughts gained a foothold. Everyone dies eventually, sooner or later. Most people die too young. The acceleration of this process here and there seemed to be a small price to pay for achieving the well-balanced, liberal world society with a high standard of living which everyone desired. Only a few surviving uneasy spirits from the 'humanitarian' epoch stubbornly went on calling it 'genocide' and 'extermination'.

From the dining room of Långbro mental hospital, I could see out over the high walls of the exercise yard, out into the grounds where I had played as a child. My wife and son, Cecilia and Aron, were allowed to come on Sundays. We used to sit on the stairs, close together.

At the time I was translating the Chinese classics. Art and meditation were merged into an indissoluble combination in my life. Some kind of transparent nebulae were pouring through my sky – immense, slow states of clarity. I saw cloudlessness assemble into cloud: condensed space.

When it was all over, I was discharged. We were living in my old family home, which was quite near the hospital. I then turned increasingly to practical magic. I was working in the basement of my childhood to root out the terror within me. I painted the walls white and the doors a lovely green. 'Even dogs are to like it here,'

I used to say. I had acquired a quiet humour which had been alien to my arrogant youth.

The basement was my garden. I equipped a little workshop there. Even if my artist's dream had been in vain, I was born with a great love of pure wood. Sometimes I sat all evening silently in the dark, as if in a cave, surrounded by the fragrant timber. I felt my life condensing into a stillness that was about to go over into complete silence.

'The world has contracted,' I occasionally thought, with a trace of a smile. It had. A 5 to 10 per cent coloured population, mainly rural, occupied with mechanized mining and agriculture in the tropical zones, was now considered to be what was technically and economically optimal. The gratitude and relief of the survivors knew no bounds. Calm and stability appeared to prevail everywhere.

In this new happy world I became more and more taciturn and introverted. My skin alone spoke, its pores opening against my will and beginning to sweat out the riches our continent had collected. A cold stinging film coated my face. The gold came pouring in from Bengal and South Africa, glittering like silver from Peru and Mexico, as intoxicating as opium. It was as white as cotton, as black as slaves, flowing like oil and coagulating like blood. It came from all times and continents and was sucked out by the capillaries of my body towards my face. Even my eyes and lips were covered. My despair was hidden beneath a golden shell.

I no longer moved, but my thoughts surrounded me like hovering birds. I seemed to be enclosed in a golden peace as if behind the eyelids of a sleeping man. It was, they said, the joy of the spirit surrounding me with its impenetrable protective film. The art I had practised was nothing but gold dust brushed over reality to fix it. Below the surface was a living human being. Anyone listening could hear his heart beating.

List of People Mentioned in *The Myth of Wu Tao-tzu*

Arendt, Hannah (1906–75), German-born American philosopher and political theorist, author of *Eichmann in Jerusalem* (1963)

Carnap, Rudolf (1891–1970), German-born American philosopher

Cliff, Mrs, a character in Sven Lindqvist's 1959 book *Hemmaresan* (*Journey at Home*)

Confucius (551–479 BC), Chinese philosopher

Ekelund, Vilhelm (1880–1949), Swedish poet and essayist. Lindqvist's postgraduate study of Ekelund's diary was published as *Dagbok och diktverk* (1966)

Fenollosa, Ernest (1853–1908), American professor of philosophy and political economy at Tokyo Imperial University whose influential essay 'The Chinese Written Character as a Medium for Poetry' was edited by Ezra Pound (1936)

Gandhi, Mohandas (1869–1948), leading personality in India's fight for independence from the British Empire

Goethe, Johann Wolfgang von (1749–1832), German poet and playwright

Goldwater, Barry (1909–98), American Republican politician

Hesse, Hermann (1877–1962), German-Swiss novelist, poet and painter

Kahn, Herman (1922–83), American military strategist, author of *Thinking about the Unthinkable* (1962)

Karlgren, Bernhard (1889–1978), Swedish sinologist and linguist, author of *Grammatica Serica Recensa* (1957), a dictionary of Old Chinese, explaining the etymology of the Chinese characters. Lindqvist followed Karlgren's seminars 1958–60

Keyser, Cassius J. (1862–1947), American mathematician, author of *Mathematical Philosophy: A Study of Fate and Freedom* (1922)

Klee, Paul (1879–1940), Swiss painter, author of *Das bildnerische Denken* (1956), published in English as *The Thinking Eye* (1961)

Lao Tse (6th century BC), Chinese philosopher

Laski, Harold (1893–1950), English political scientist and socialist

Leibniz, Gottfried Wilhelm (1646–1716), German philosopher and mathematician

London, Jack (1876–1916), American writer who tried living as a poor man among the poorest in the East End slums of London, reporting his experiment in *The People of the Abyss* (1903)

Lundkvist, Artur (1906–91), Swedish poet and travel writer whose *Indiabrand* (1950) described an India in need of revolution

Moore, G. E. (1873–1958), English philosopher

Musil, Robert (1880–1942), Austrian novelist, author of *Der Mann ohne Eigenschaften* (1930–34), translated as *The Man Without Qualities* (1953–61)

THE MYTH OF WU TAO-TZU

Needham, Joseph (1900–95), English biochemist and historian of Chinese science who initiated the series *Science and Civilization in China* (1954–)

Nehru, Jawaharlal (1889–1964), first prime minister of independent India

Poincaré, Henri (1854–1912), French mathematician

Pound, Ezra (1885–1972), American poet and author of *Guide to Kulchur*

Proust, Marcel (1871–1922), French novelist

Russell, Bertrand (1872–1970), British philosopher and mathematician, lectured in China 1920–21

Ruysbroek, Jan van (1293–1381), Flemish mystic

Ruysbroek, Willem van (*c.* 1220–*c.* 1270), Flemish Franciscan monk who undertook a mission to, and then wrote one of the earliest Western accounts of, the Mongols

Schiller, Friedrich von (1759–1805), German dramatist, poet and historian

Shakespeare, William (1564–1616), English playwright and poet

Sirén, Osvald (1879–1966), Swedish art historian, author of *Chinese Painting: Leading Masters and Principles* (7 vols., 1956–8)

Smith, Ian (1919–2007), Rhodesian prime minister who resisted black majority rule

Spengler, Oswald (1880–1936), German historian and philosopher, author of *Der Untergang des Abendlandes* (1918–22)

Stifter, Adalbert (1805–68), Austrian writer, poet and painter

Tagore, Rabindranath (1861–1941), Indian poet and philosopher

Tingsten, Herbert (1896–1973), Swedish political scientist and journalist whose *Problemet Sydafrika* (*The Problem of South Africa*) was published in 1954

Tolstoy, Leo (1828–1910), Russian novelist

Tortsov, Konstantin Stanislavski's alter ego in his book *An Actor Prepares* (1936)

Vorster, Balthazar Johannes (1915–83), South African politician and prime minister during the apartheid era

Wallace, George (1919–98), American politician who favoured racial segregation

Wittgenstein, Ludwig (1889–1951), Austrian-born Cambridge philosopher

Wu Tao-tzu (7th century AD), Tang Dynasty Chinese artist renowned for his murals on temple and monastery walls in Chang'an and Lo Yang